Fear of Knowledge

Fear of Knowledge

Against Relativism and Constructivism

Paul A. Boghossian

CLARENDON PRESS · OXFORD

OXFORD
UNIVERSITY PRESS

Great Clarendon Street, Oxford OX2 6DP

Oxford University Press is a department of the University of Oxford.
It furthers the University's objective of excellence in research, scholarship,
and education by publishing worldwide in

Oxford New York

Auckland Cape Town Dar es Salaam Hong Kong Karachi
Kuala Lumpur Madrid Melbourne Mexico City Nairobi
New Delhi Shanghai Taipei Toronto

With offices in

Argentina Austria Brazil Chile Czech Republic France Greece
Guatemala Hungary Italy Japan Poland Portugal
Singapore South Korea Switzerland Thailand Turkey Ukraine Vietnam

Oxford is a registered trade mark of Oxford University Press
in the UK and in certain other countries

Published in the United States
by Oxford University Press Inc., New York

British Library Cataloguing in Publication Data
Data available

Library of Congress Cataloging in Publication Data
Data available

Typeset by SPI Publisher Services, Pondicherry, India
Printed in Great Britain
on acid-free paper by
Biddles Ltd., King's Lynn, Norfolk

ISBN 0-19-928718-x   978- 0-19-928718-5

For my mother,
Méliné Yalenezian Boghossian

PREFACE

It is rare for a philosophical idea to command widespread acceptance in the broader intellectual community of the academy; philosophy, by its nature, tends towards claims of a scope and generality that invite controversy.

Over the past twenty years or so, however, a remarkable consensus has formed—in the human and social sciences, even if not in the natural sciences—around a thesis about the nature of human knowledge. It is the thesis that knowledge is socially constructed.

Although the terminology of social construction is relatively recent, the underlying ideas, as we shall see, engage long-standing issues about the relation between mind and reality, issues that first attracted me to philosophy itself.

If this book appears to pay disproportionate attention to the work of Richard Rorty that is not only because of Rorty's huge influence on contemporary constructivist views, but also because, as a first-year graduate student at Princeton in 1979, I first came to appreciate the power of these views in a seminar of his. Although they clashed with the strongly objectivist tendencies I had brought to graduate school from my undergraduate education in physics, I found the arguments for at least some constructivist theses—the ones concerning rational belief—disquieting, and thought that academic philosophy had been too quick to dismiss them. I have always been grateful to Rorty for having made me see the need to engage these ideas.

Because the issues it addresses have come to attract a wide audience, I have tried to make this book accessible not only to professional philosophers but to anyone who values serious argument. While I don't know how well I have succeeded, I do know that I radically underestimated how difficult a task that would be.

As a result, this book has taken longer to write than I ever expected. Along the way, I have benefited from the comments of a large number of friends, colleagues and students, among whom I should especially mention: Ned Block, Jennifer Church, Stewart Cohen, Annalisa Coliva, Paolo Faria, Abouali Farmanfarmaian, Kit Fine, Allan Gibbard, Anthony Gottlieb, Elizabeth Harman, Paul Horwich, Paolo Leonardi, Michael Lynch, Anna Sara Malmgren, Thomas Nagel, Ram Neta, Derek Parfit, James Pryor, Stephen Schiffer, Nishiten Shah, Alan Sokal, Dan Sperber, David Velleman, Roger White and an anonymous referee for Oxford University Press. Thanks to Michael Steinberg for aesthetic advice, David James Barnett for preparing the index and Joshua Schechter for closely vetting the manuscript and for many hours of enjoyable conversations about these and other topics. I owe a special debt of gratitude to Dean Richard Foley, Provost David McLanghlin and President John Sexton for their support not only of my research but of the wonderful philosophy department at NYU. Finally, I am grateful to Tamsin Shaw for her encouragement and advice.

CONTENTS

I

Introduction

Equal Validity

ON October 22, 1996, *The New York Times* ran an unusual front-page story. Entitled "Indian Tribes' Creationists Thwart Archeologists," it described a conflict that had arisen between two views of where Native American populations originated. According to the standard, extensively confirmed archaeological account, humans first entered the Americas from Asia, crossing the Bering Strait some 10,000 years ago. By contrast, some Native American creation myths hold that native peoples have lived in the Americas ever since their ancestors first emerged onto the surface of the earth from a subterranean world of spirits. As Sebastian LeBeau, an official of the Cheyenne River Sioux, a Lakota tribe based in Eagle Butte, S.D., put it:

We know where we came from. We are the descendants of the Buffalo people. They came from inside the earth after supernatural spirits prepared this world for humankind to live here. If non-Indians choose to believe they evolved from an ape, so be it. I have yet to come across five Lakotas who believe in science and in evolution.

The *Times* went on to note that many archeologists, torn between their commitment to scientific method and their appreciation for native culture, "have been driven close to a postmodern relativism in which science is just one more belief system." Roger Anyon, a British archeologist who has worked for the Zuni people, was quoted as saying:

Science is just one of many ways of knowing the world. [The Zunis' world view is] just as valid as the archeological viewpoint of what prehistory is about.

Another archeologist, Dr Larry Zimmerman, of the University of Iowa, was quoted as calling for a

different kind of science, between the boundaries of Western ways of knowing and Indian ways of knowing.

Dr Zimmerman added:

I personally do reject science as a privileged way of seeing the world.

Arresting as these remarks are, they would be of only passing interest were it not for the enormous influence of the general philosophical perspective they represent. Especially within the academy, but also and inevitably to some extent outside of it, the idea that there are "many equally valid ways of knowing the world," with science being just one of them, has taken very deep root. In vast stretches of the humanities and social sciences, this sort of "postmodernist relativism" about knowledge has achieved the status of orthodoxy. I shall call it (as neutrally as possible) the doctrine of

Equal Validity:
There are many radically different, yet "equally valid" ways of knowing the world, with science being just one of them.

Here are a few representative examples of scholars endorsing the basic thought behind equal validity:

As we come to recognize the conventional and artifactual status of our forms of knowing, we put ourselves in a position to realize that it is ourselves and not reality that is responsible for what we know.[1]

First-world science is one science among many... [2]

For the relativist there is no sense attached to the idea that some standards or beliefs are really rational as distinct from merely locally accepted as such. Because he thinks that there are no context-free or super-cultural norms of rationality he does not see rationally and irrationally held beliefs as making up two distinct and qualitatively different classes of thing.[3]

There are many more such passages that could be cited.

What is it about the doctrine of equal validity that seems so radical and counterintuitive?

Well, ordinarily, we think that on a factual question like the one about American prehistory, there is a way things are that is independent of us and our beliefs about it—an *objective* fact of the matter, as we may put it, as to where the first Americans originated.

We are not necessarily *fact-objectivists* in this sense about *all* domains of judgment. About morality, for example, some people, philosophers included, are inclined to be relativists: they hold that there are many alternative moral codes specifying what counts as good or bad conduct, but no facts by virtue of which some of these codes are more 'correct' than any of the others.[4] Others may be relativists about aesthetics, about what

[1] Steven Shapin and Simon Schaffer, *Leviathan and the Air-Pump: Hobbes, Boyle, and the Experimental Life* (Princeton: Princeton University Press, 1985).

[2] Paul Feyerabend, Introduction to the Chinese edition of *Against Method*, reproduced in Paul Feyerabend, *Against Method*, 3 edn. (New York: Verso, 1993), 3, emphasis in original; quoted in Alan Sokal and Jean Bricmont, *Fashionable Nonsense: Postmodern Intellectuals' Abuse of Science* (New York: Picador USA, 1998), 85.

[3] Barry Barnes and David Bloor, "Relativism, Rationalism and the Sociology of Knowledge," in *Rationality and Relativism*, ed. by Martin Hollis and Steven Lukes (Cambridge, Mass.: The MIT Press, 1982), 21–47.

[4] For a defense of moral relativism, see Gilbert Harman's contribution to Gilbert Harman and Judith Jarvis Thomson, *Moral Relativism and Moral Objectivity* (Cambridge, Mass.: Blackwell Publishers, 1996).

counts as beautiful or artistically valuable. These sorts of relativism about value matters are debatable, of course, and still debated. However, even if we find them ultimately implausible, they do not immediately strike us as absurd. But on a factual question such as the one about the origins of the first Americans, we are inclined to think, surely, there just is some objective fact of the matter.

We may not know what this fact of the matter is, but, having formed an interest in the question, we seek to know it. And we have a variety of techniques and methods—observation, logic, inference to the best explanation and so forth, but not tea-leaf reading or crystal ball gazing—that we take to be the only legitimate ways of forming rational beliefs on the subject. These methods—the methods characteristic of what we call 'science' but which also characterize ordinary modes of knowledge-seeking—have led us to the view that the first Americans came from Asia across the Bering Strait. This view may be false, of course, but it is the most reasonable one, given the evidence— or so we are ordinarily tempted to think.

Because we believe all this, we *defer* to the deliverances of science: we assign it a privileged role in determining what to teach our children at school, what to accept as probative in our courts of law and what to base our social policies upon. We take there to be a fact of the matter as to what is true. We want to accept only what there is good reason to believe true; and we take science to be the only good way to arrive at reasonable beliefs about what is true, at least in the realm of the purely factual. Hence, we defer to science.

For this sort of deference to science to be right, however, scientific knowledge had better *be* privileged—it had better not be the case that there are many other, radically different yet equally valid ways of knowing the world, with science being just one of them. For if science wasn't privileged, we might well have to accord as much credibility to archeology as to

Zuni creationism, as much credibility to evolution as to Christian creationism—precisely the view advocated by an increasing number of scholars in the academy, and increasingly echoed by people outside it.[5]

Equal validity, then, is a doctrine of considerable significance, and not just within the confines of the ivory tower. If the vast numbers of scholars in the humanities and social sciences who subscribe to it are right, we are not merely making a philosophical mistake of interest to a small number of specialists in the theory of knowledge; we have fundamentally misconceived the principles by which society ought to be organized. There is more than the usual urgency, then, to the question whether they are right.

The Social Construction of Knowledge

How did so many contemporary scholars come to be convinced of a doctrine as radical and as counterintuitive as equal validity?

It's an interesting question whether the explanation for this development is primarily intellectual or ideological in nature; there is undoubtedly an element of each.

Ideologically, the appeal of the doctrine of equal validity cannot be detached from its emergence in the post-colonial era. Advocates of colonial expansion often sought to justify their projects by the claim that colonized subjects stood to gain much from the superior science and culture of the West. In a moral climate which has turned its back decisively on colonialism, it is appealing to many to say not only—what is true—that one cannot morally justify subjugating a sovereign people in the name of spreading knowledge, but that there is no such thing as superior

---

[5] Footnote for the wary reader: In the interest of setting up the issues that will concern me, I am moving rather quickly over some tricky terrain. Important distinctions and qualifications will be introduced below.

knowledge only different knowledges, each appropriate to its own particular setting.

Intellectually speaking, the appeal of equal validity appears to derive from the conviction of many scholars that the best philosophical thought of our time has swept aside the intuitive objectivist conceptions of truth and rationality that I gestured at above and had replaced them with conceptions of knowledge that vindicate equal validity. What are these conceptions?

The idea at the core of these new 'postmodern' conceptions of knowledge is concisely expressed in the following passage:

Feminist epistemologists, in common with many other strands of contemporary epistemology, no longer regard knowledge as a neutral transparent reflection of an independently existing reality, with truth and falsity established by transcendent procedures of rational assessment. Rather, most accept that all knowledge is situated knowledge, reflecting the position of the knowledge producer at a certain historical moment in a given material and cultural context.[6]

According to this core idea, the truth of a belief is not a matter of how things stand with an "independently existing reality;" and its rationality is not a matter of its approval by "transcendent procedures of rational assessment." Rather, whether a belief is knowledge necessarily depends at least in part on the contingent social and material setting in which that belief is produced (or maintained). I shall call any conception of knowledge which incorporates this core conviction a *social dependence* conception of knowledge.

In recent times, the most influential versions of social dependence views of knowledge have been formulated in terms of the now ubiquitous notion of *social construction*. All knowledge, it is said, is socially dependent because all knowledge is socially

---

[6] Kathleen Lennon, "Feminist Epistemology as Local Epistemology," *Proceedings of the Aristotelian Society, Supplementary Volume* 71 (1997): 37.

constructed. In what follows, therefore, I shall be especially interested in *social constructivist* conceptions of knowledge.

Regardless, however, of how the social dependence of knowledge is ultimately grounded, it should be immediately clear how such a conception of knowledge could help vindicate equal validity, were it to be accepted. If a belief's being knowledge is always a function of the contingent social setting in which it is produced, then it looks as though it could very well turn out that what is knowledge for us is not knowledge for the Zunis, despite our having access to all the same information (more on this below).

Philosophy in the Academy

I have emphasized the influence that constructivist ideas currently exert in the humanities and social sciences. But there is one humanities discipline in which their hold is actually quite weak, and that is in philosophy itself, at least as it is practiced within the mainstream of analytic philosophy departments within the English-speaking world.

That is not to say that such ideas have received no support from analytic philosophers. On the contrary, one could cite a sizeable proportion of that tradition's most prominent philosophers in their defense—Ludwig Wittgenstein, Rudolf Carnap, Richard Rorty, Thomas Kuhn, Hilary Putnam and Nelson Goodman, just for example. These philosophers in turn could appeal to some important intellectual precedents.

Immanuel Kant famously denied that the world, insofar as we can know it, could be independent of the concepts in terms of which we grasp it. David Hume questioned our right to think that there is some uniquely correct set of epistemic principles that capture what it is for a belief to be rationally held. And Friedrich Nietzsche can be read as wondering whether we are ever really moved to belief by evidence, as opposed to the various other non-epistemic motives—self-interest or ideology—that could be acting upon us.

But for all their distinguished intellectual pedigree and for all the attention they have received in recent times, it remains fair to say that such anti-objectivist conceptions of truth and rationality are not generally accepted within the mainstream of philosophy departments within the English-speaking world.

The result has been a growing alienation of academic philosophy from the rest of the humanities and social sciences, leading to levels of acrimony and tension on American campuses that have prompted the label "Science Wars."

Scholars sympathetic to postmodernism complain that the case for revising traditional conceptions of knowledge has been overwhelmingly clear for quite some time, and nothing but the usual intransigence of established orthodoxy can explain the resistance with which these new ideas have been greeted.[7] Traditionalists, on the other hand, have impatiently dismissed their philosophically minded colleagues in the humanities and social sciences as motivated more by considerations of political correctness than by genuine philosophical insight.[8]

It is against this backdrop that I write the present book. My aim is to clarify what is at issue between constructivism and its

[7] See, for example, Barbara Herrnstein Smith, "Cutting-Edge Equivocation: Conceptual Moves and Rhetorical Strategies in Contemporary Anti-Epistemology," *South Atlantic Quarterly* 101, no. 1 (2002): 187–212.

[8] One of their number, Alan Sokal, a physicist by profession who moonlights as an anti-relativist philosopher of science, went so far as to submit to a leading cultural studies journal a parody article crammed with scientific and philosophical howlers. Unfortunately for the postmodernist camp, his preposterously entitled article was published by that journal with some fanfare. See Alan Sokal, "Transgressing the Boundaries: Towards a Transformative Hermeneutics of Quantum Gravity," *Social Text* 46/7 (1996): 217–52 and Paul Boghossian, "What the Sokal Hoax Ought to Teach Us," *Times Literary Supplement*, December 13, 1996, 14–15. For further discussion of Sokal's hoax, see The Editors of *Lingua Franca*, ed., *The Sokal Hoax: The Sham that Shook the Academy* (Lincoln, Nebr.: University of Nebraska Press, 2000).

critics, and to map the terrain in which these issues are embedded. My ambition is not to be exhaustive, examining every view that the literature has thrown up or every argument that has been advocated. Instead, I will isolate the three theses that, as it seems to me, a constructivism about knowledge could most interestingly amount to. And I will then attempt to assess their plausibility.

The first thesis will be a constructivism about truth; the second a constructivism about justification; and the third, finally, will concern the role of social factors in explaining why we believe what we believe.

Since each of these theses has an important and complex philosophical history, it would be unreasonable to expect a definitive assessment of their truth or falsity in this short book. I will attempt to show, however, that each of them is subject to very powerful objections, objections that help explain why contemporary analytic philosophers continue to reject them.

2

The Social Construction of Knowledge

Belief, Facts and Truth

BEFORE proceeding any further, it will be useful to lay down some terminology for the systematic description of our cognitive activities.

I have been talking about the Zunis believing this and our believing that. What is it for someone to believe something?

A belief is a particular kind of mental state. If we ask precisely what kind of mental state it is, we find that it is not easy to say. We can describe it in other words, of course, but only in ones that cry out for as much explanation as talk about belief. To believe that Jupiter has sixteen moons, we could say, is to *take* the world to be such that in it Jupiter has sixteen moons; or to *represent* the world as containing a particular heavenly body with sixteen moons; and so forth.

Although we may not be able to analyze belief in terms of significantly other concepts, we can see clearly that three aspects are essential to it. Any belief must have a propositional *content*;

any belief can be assessed as *true or false*; and any belief can be assessed as *justified or unjustified, rational or irrational*.

Consider Margo's belief that Jupiter has sixteen moons. We attribute this belief with the sentence:

Margo believes that Jupiter has sixteen moons.

That Jupiter has sixteen moons, we may say, is the *propositional content* of what Margo believes.

The propositional content of a belief specifies how the world is according to the belief. It specifies, in other words, a *truth condition*—how the world would have to be if the belief is to be true. Thus,

Margo's belief that Jupiter has sixteen moons is true if and only if Jupiter has sixteen moons

As we may also put it, Margo's belief is true if and only if it is a *fact* that Jupiter has sixteen moons.

In general, then, we can say that

S's belief that p is true if and only if p

with the left-hand side of this biconditional attributing truth to a belief with a given content, and the right-hand side describing the fact that would have to obtain if the attribution is to be true.

A propositional content (or proposition, for short) is built up out of *concepts*. So, for someone to be able to believe the proposition that Jupiter has sixteen moons, they must *have* the concepts out of which that particular proposition is built, namely, the concept *Jupiter*, the concept *having*, the concept *sixteen*, and the concept *moon*.[1]

---

[1] A word in quotes will serve, as usual, to designate that word; a word italicized and in bold will serve to designate the concept expressed by that word. This view of propositions is broadly Fregean. It is the view that I favor. However, none of the arguments in this book will depend crucially on whether we opt for a Fregean as opposed to a Millian view of propositions, according to which the constituents of propositions are not concepts but rather worldly items, such as Jupiter itself. For more on this distinction see Saul Kripke, *Naming and Necessity* (Cambridge, Mass.: Harvard University Press, 1980).

This gives us yet another, equivalent, way to talk about the truth of a belief. We could equally say that the belief that Jupiter has sixteen moons is true just in case the entity referred to by the concept in the subject position—namely, the concept *Jupiter*—has the property denoted by the concept in the object position—namely, the concept **has sixteen moons**. Since the entity in question doesn't have the property at issue—Jupiter, it turns out, has over thirty moons—the belief is false.

Universality, Objectivity and Mind-Independence

I have just asserted that Jupiter has over thirty moons. Obviously, my saying it is so doesn't automatically make it so, otherwise there could not be any such thing as false assertion. If my assertion is true it is because, in addition to my saying it, it's a *fact* that Jupiter has over thirty moons. Well, let us suppose that my assertion is true—that is, that the corresponding fact obtains.

Here's an interesting question: Does it follow from its being a fact that Jupiter has over thirty moons that *it's a fact for everyone* that Jupiter has over thirty moons, that it's a fact for all communities?

Well, it depends what one means by the phrase "it's a fact for everyone." It is certainly not a fact for everyone in the sense that everyone believes the proposition that Jupiter has over thirty moons. Some may never have considered the question; others may have come to the opposite conclusion. So, in the utterly trivial sense in which I may believe in a fact while others don't, some facts are facts for me but not for others.

But if what we mean is something more ambitious—that the fact that Jupiter has over thirty moons can somehow "hold" for me but not for you, that seems harder to comprehend. After all, my belief is not in the proposition

Jupiter has over thirty moons for me

but, rather, in the impersonal proposition

Jupiter has over thirty moons.

So, if we say that that belief is true, then it looks as though the corresponding fact has to obtain for everyone, whether they are inclined to believe it or not.

Intuitively, then, the fact that Jupiter has over thirty moons is a *universal* fact—it does not vary from person to person or community to community.

By contrast, the fact that slurping your noodles is rude is not a universal fact: it holds in the US but not in Japan (how exactly to formulate this variability will concern us later).

In the case of Jupiter's having over thirty moons, we can go further: it's not merely that it looks to be universal, it also looks to be completely *mind-independent*: it would have obtained even if human beings had never existed.

By contrast, the fact that there is money in the world is not a mind-independent fact—money could not have existed without persons and their intentions to exchange goods with one another.

Universality and mind-independence, then, are two important notions of "objectivity." We can also introduce more specific notions. For example, we can ask whether in addition to being mind-dependent a given fact is *belief*-dependent—does it depend on someone's *believing* it? We can ask whether in addition to being mind-dependent a given fact is *society*-dependent—could it only have obtained in the context of a group of human beings organized in a particular way? In what follows, I will always indicate which of these notions of objectivity is at stake in any particular dispute.

Rational Belief

Let us go back to the discussion of belief. Beliefs, we have said, can be assessed as true or false. But they can also be assessed along a second dimension. If Margo tells us that Jupiter has sixteen moons we will want to know whether she is *justified* in believing this, or whether this is just a number she has pulled out of a hat. Does she have *reasons* that make it *rational* for her to believe it?[2]

What do we mean by a reason for belief? Ordinarily, we have in mind *evidence* for the belief, a consideration or observation that increases the likelihood of the truth of the belief. Here we could imagine that Margo is an astronomer who has trained her powerful telescope on Jupiter and has counted its various moons. Let us call such reasons *epistemic* reasons.

Some philosophers have thought that there can also be *non-epistemic* reasons for believing a given proposition. Many religious conversions were achieved at the point of a gun: "Believe this or else . . . ." A person staring down a gun barrel could be thought to have reason to adopt whatever creed was being promoted—a *pragmatic* reason, if not an *epistemic* one: the considerations offered don't speak to the belief's truth only to the pragmatic advantages of having it (not getting your head blown off).

This distinction—between epistemic and pragmatic reasons for belief—is illustrated by Blaise Pascal's famous argument to the effect that we all have reason to believe in God. Pascal's point was that the consequences of failing to believe in Him if he exists (eternal hell fire and damnation) are much worse than the consequences of believing in Him if he does not (a certain amount of sin-avoidance and contrition). Hence, it is better on the whole to believe than not. If the argument worked, at most it would establish that we have a pragmatic reason for believing in God, not an epistemic one, for the argument does nothing to further the likelihood that the Almighty exists. By contrast, we commonly take astronomical observations of Jupiter to provide us with epistemic, not pragmatic, reasons for believing that it has a certain number of moons.

---

[2] I shall be using the notions "justified" and "rational" interchangeably.

We have said that Margo's being *rational* in believing that Jupiter has sixteen moons involves her having good reasons for that belief. But are we talking here about *epistemic* reasons or might other sorts of reasons enter into rationality as well, such as pragmatic ones?

We shall come back to this question. As we shall see, one of the views that we shall want to consider at length is the view that rationality is always partly a matter of a person's *non-epistemic* reasons.

However we end up construing rationality, notice that reasons for belief are *fallible*: one can have good reasons to believe something false. The evidence available to pre-Aristotelian Greeks made it rational for them to believe that earth was flat, even though as we may now be said to know, it is round.

As this example also shows, reasons are *defeasible*: one can have good reasons to believe something at one time and then, as a result of further information, cease to have good reasons to believe that same proposition at some later time. The pre-Aristotelian Greeks justifiably believed earth to be flat; we justifiably believe it to be round.

Suppose, then, that as visual observations of the earth from space seem decisively to confirm, this planet we live on *is* in fact round. Then our belief that it is round is both justified and true; according to the standard, widely accepted Platonic definition of knowledge, then, our belief counts as *knowledge*.

Knowledge:

A thinker S knows that p if and only if:

1. S believes p
2. S is justified in believing p
3. p is true.

Our early ancestors *thought* they knew that earth was flat, but they were wrong. Although their belief about earth was justified, it was false. If a belief is to count as knowledge, it must not only be justified; it must also be true.[3]

Social Construction

Armed with this understanding of some of the central concepts in the theory of knowledge, we are now in a position to ask what it could mean to say that knowledge is socially constructed.

Few notions have achieved greater prominence in the contemporary academy than the notion of social construction. In his recent book, *The Social Construction of What?*, Ian Hacking lists over fifty kinds of item that, in addition to facts, knowledge and reality, have been claimed to be socially constructed—including, authorship, brotherhood, the child viewer of television, emotions, homosexual culture, illness, the medicalized immigrant, quarks, urban schooling and Zulu nationalism. And his list is far from comprehensive.[4]

Our interest is in the claim that knowledge is socially constructed. Before we tackle that question, however, let us begin by asking more generally what it means to say of something—anything—that it is socially constructed.

Ordinarily, to say that something is *constructed* is to say that it was not there simply to be *found* or discovered, but rather that it was *built*, brought into being by some person's intentional activity at a given point in time. And to say that it was *socially* constructed is to add that it was built by a society, by a group of people organized in a particular way, with particular values, interests and needs.

[3] There are some well-known counterexamples to this definition, first devised by Edmund Gettier. See Edmund Gettier, "Is Justified True Belief Knowledge?," *Analysis* 23 (1963): 121–3. The complications that result will not concern us.

[4] See Ian Hacking, *The Social Construction of What?* (Cambridge, Mass.: Harvard University Press, 1999), 1–2.

There are three important respects in which a social construction theorist of the kind that we are currently interested in departs from, or adds to, this perfectly ordinary notion of social construction.

First, in the ordinary sense, it is typically *things* or *objects* that are constructed, like houses or chairs; but our theorist is interested not so much in the construction of things as in the construction of *facts*—in the fact that some piece of metal is a coin rather than in the piece of metal itself.

Second, our social construction theorist is not interested in cases where, *as a matter of contingent fact*, some fact is brought into being by the intentional activities of persons, but only in cases where such facts could *only* have been brought into being in that way. In the intended technical sense, in other words, it has to be *constitutive* of a given fact that it was created by a society if it is to be called "socially constructed."

In the ordinary sense, if a group of people gather together to move a heavy boulder to the top of a hill, we would have to say that the boulder's resting on top of the hill is a socially constructed fact. In the more demanding technical sense of the theorist, the boulder's resting on top of the hill is not a socially constructed fact for it could have come about through purely natural forces.

On the other hand, a piece of paper's being money is a socially constructed fact in the technical sense, for it is necessarily true that it could only have come to be money by being used in certain ways by human beings organized as a social group.

Finally, a typical social construction claim will involve not merely the claim that a particular fact was built by a social group, but that it was constructed in a way that reflects their *contingent* needs and interests, so that had they not had those needs and interests they might well not have constructed that fact. The ordinary notion of a constructed fact is perfectly compatible with the idea that a particular construction was forced, that we had no choice but to construct that fact. According to Kant, for example, the world we experience is constructed by our minds to obey certain fundamental laws, among them the laws of geometry and arithmetic. But Kant didn't think we were free to do otherwise. On the contrary, he thought that any conscious mind was constrained to construct a world which obeys those laws.[5]

The social construction theorist is not typically interested in such mandated constructions. He wants to emphasize the *contingency* of the facts we have constructed, to show that they needn't have obtained had we chosen otherwise.

In the intended technical sense, then, a fact is socially constructed if and only if it is *necessarily true* that it could only have obtained through the contingent actions of a social group. Henceforth, when I talk of social construction, I shall mean it in this technical sense.

There would, of course, be precious little point in writing a book revealing that facts about money or citizenship are social constructs, for that much is obvious. A social construction claim is interesting only insofar as it purports to expose construction where none had been suspected, where something constitutively social had come to masquerade as natural. But that pushes the question back: Why is it of such great interest to expose construction wherever it exists?

According to Hacking, the interest derives from the following simple thought. If some fact belongs to a species of natural fact, then we are simply stuck with facts of that kind. However, if facts of the relevant kind are in fact social constructions, then they need not have obtained had we not wished them to obtain. Thus, exposure of social construction is potentially liberating: a kind of fact that had come to seem inevitable would have been unmasked (in Hacking's apt term) as a contingent social development.

[5] See Immanuel Kant, *Critique of Pure Reason*, trans. Norman Kemp Smith, (New York: Macmillan, 1929).

This line of thought is overly simple in at least two respects. First, it is not true that if something is a natural fact that we are simply stuck with it. Polio is a purely natural disease, but it could have been eradicated and almost was. The course of the Colorado River is the result of purely natural forces, but it was possible to transform it through the construction of a dam. Many species have become extinct and many others are expected to become so.

Second, consider a case—like that of money—in which it *is* true that had we chosen not to construct it, it would not have existed. This does suggest that, if we wished, we could make it the case that there ceases to be money in the future (although it would obviously be far from easy). But we cannot undo the past. Given that it is now true that there is money, no amount of our choosing to do things differently in the future can make it the case that there never was any money.

With these two important qualifications in place, we may endorse Hacking's basic claim.

The Constructivist Picture of Knowledge

Let us turn now to the question what it might mean to say that *knowledge* is socially constructed. Consider something that we now take ourselves to know—for example, that dinosaurs once roamed the earth—and suppose that we actually know it. What surprising dependence on contingent social needs and interests does the social constructivist claim to have discovered in this item of knowledge?

Although there have been many interesting controversies about the notion of knowledge, there is a broad consensus among philosophers, from Aristotle to the present day, on the nature of the relationship between knowledge and the contingent social circumstances in which it is produced. I shall refer to this consensus as the 'classical picture of knowledge.'

According to this picture, there are several respects in which no one should deny that the enterprise of knowledge may exhibit an important social dimension. No one should deny, for example, that knowledge is often produced collaboratively, by members of a social group, and that contingent facts about that group may explain why it shows an interest in certain questions over others. It's an interesting empirical question to what extent sheer curiosity about the truth is simply built into our biological make-up and to what extent it is a product of our social development. In any case, it is easy to imagine a society that did not care about the ancient past or that did not think it a useful expenditure of its resources to find out about it, given other pressing needs much closer to home.

Similarly, the classical picture does not deny that the members of a knowledge-seeking group may have certain political and social values and that those values *may* influence how they conduct their work—what observations they make and how well they appraise the evidence that they encounter. It forms no part of the classical conception of knowledge to deny that inquirers may be *biased* by their background values into believing claims for which there is no evidence. So, our interest in certain questions over others and the integrity with which we pursue them—both of these important domains are clearly not independent of the kind of society we are.

The respects in which the classical picture insists on the independence of knowledge from contingent social circumstance have to do, rather, with three different claims.

First, and perhaps most importantly, the classical conception holds that many *facts* about the world are independent of us, and hence independent of our social values and interests. For example, according to the classical conception, the *fact* (assuming it to be a fact for the moment) that dinosaurs once roamed the earth is not dependent on us but is, rather, just a natural fact that obtains without any help from us.

The second aspect of the classical conception that's of interest concerns not truth but our *justification* for believing that something is true. The point is somewhat subtle. We have already seen that, in an important sense, it is not inevitable that we should have shown an interest in the ancient past, or that, having shown an interest in it, we should have stumbled across the fossil record that attests to the existence of the dinosaurs. So, neither of those facts is independent of our social make-up.

However, according to the classical picture, what *is* independent of our social make-up is the fact that the fossil record we have discovered constitutes *evidence* for the existence of dinosaurs— contributes to making it rational, in other words, to believe in their existence. That we should have discovered the evidence for the dinosaurs may not be independent of our social context; but *that it is evidence* for that hypothesis is.

The third and final aspect of the classical conception that is of importance to us concerns the role of epistemic reasons in *explaining* why we believe what we believe. According to the classical picture, our exposure to the *evidence* for believing that there were dinosaurs can, on occasion, by itself suffice to explain *why* we believe that there were dinosaurs; we do not always need to invoke other factors, and, in particular, do not need to invoke our contingent social values and interests.

Once again, it is important to guard against misunderstanding. I have already emphasized that social factors may have to enter into an explanation of why we show an interest in a particular question and of how diligently we pursue it. However, given an interest in the question, and given our exposure to the relevant evidence, then, according to the classical picture, it is sometimes *possible* for the evidence alone to explain why we came to believe what we did.

This is not to deny, as we have just conceded above, that there may be cases where what explains our belief is something *non-evidential*; the classical picture has no interest in denying the existence of episodes in the history of inquiry where scientists may have jumped to conclusions, or allowed their career interests to cloud their better judgment. It is simply to insist that this need not *always* be so, that it is *possible* for our epistemic reasons alone to explain why we believe what we do.

We may sum up the classical picture of knowledge, then, in the following three theses.

The Classical Picture of Knowledge:

Objectivism about Facts: The world which we seek to understand and know about is what it is largely independently of us and our beliefs about it. Even if thinking beings had never existed, the world would still have had many of the properties that it currently has.

Objectivism about Justification: Facts of the form—information E justifies belief B—are society-independent facts. In particular, whether or not some item of information justifies a given belief does not depend on the contingent needs and interests of any community.

Objectivism about Rational Explanation: Under the appropriate circumstances, our exposure to the evidence alone is capable of explaining why we believe what we believe.

Different versions of constructivism take issue with one or another of these claims, and sometimes with all three at once.

Constructivism about Knowledge:

Constructivism about Facts: The world which we seek to understand and know about is not what it is independently of us and our social context; rather, all facts are socially constructed in a way that reflects our contingent needs and interests.

Constructivism about Justification: Facts of the form—information E justifies belief B—are not what they are independently of us and our social context; rather, all such facts are constructed in a way that reflects our contingent needs and interests.

Constructivism about Rational Explanation: It is never possible to explain why we believe what we believe solely on the basis of our exposure to the relevant evidence; our contingent needs and interests must also be invoked.

It is obvious that the second constructivist thesis is a consequence of the first: if all facts are socially constructed, *a fortiori* so are facts about what justifies what. It is somewhat less obvious that the third constructivist thesis can be seen to be a version of the second. For suppose, as a constructivism about rational explanation would have us believe, that our epistemic reasons alone can never explain why we come to believe what we believe on a given question, that such explanations must inevitably appeal to our pragmatic reasons (our needs and interests). Well, if our exposure to the evidence can never by itself be adequate to explain why we find a given belief compelling, we can hardly be *required* to believe something solely on the basis of evidence, for we could hardly be required to do something that it is impossible for us to do. (It is a generally recognized constraint on a legitimate requirement that we ought to be able to conform to it.) It follows, therefore, on such a view, that the rationality of a belief is always in part a function of the contingent pragmatic reasons that there may be for it.

Many scholars are attracted to such constructivist conceptions of truth and rationality independently of any overt concern with the doctrine of equal validity—the view, recall, that there are many radically different yet "equally valid" ways of knowing the world, with science being just one of them. But whatever the source of their appeal, we are now in a position to lay out very clearly why equal validity will seem plausible to anyone who finds even one of these constructivist theses true.

Thus, if fact-constructivism were true, we couldn't just say that there is some fact of the matter out there about where the first Americans originated. Rather, since all facts are constructed by societies to meet their needs and interests, it could well turn out that we and the Zunis had constructed different facts, for we clearly have different social needs and interests. Hence, our two views could be equally valid because they each report accurately on the facts constructed by our respective communities. Fact-constructivism will be the topic of Chapters 3 and 4.

Next, consider a constructivist view of justification, according to which it could not simply be an objective fact about the available evidence that it supports the Bering Strait hypothesis; rather, such a fact must have been constructed by us in a way that reflects our needs and interests. On the most plausible story about how this might go, the idea is there are many different epistemic systems for assessing the relevance of information to belief and nothing that privileges some of those systems over others in point of accuracy. Thus, the fossil record at our disposal might count as evidence for the Bering Strait hypothesis for us, given the epistemic system we find it useful to employ, but not for the Zunis, who employ a different system which suits their purposes better. Constructivism about justification will be discussed in Chapters 5, 6 and 7.

Finally, suppose, as a constructivism about rational explanation would have us think, that the rationality of a belief is always in part a function of the pragmatic reasons that there may be for it. Given the difference between our social values and interests and those of the Zunis, it may well turn out that it is pragmatic and hence rational for us to believe one thing and pragmatic and hence rational for them to believe another, even while we keep our exposure to all the relevant evidence fixed. We will assess the plausibility of this view in Chapter 8.

3

Constructing the Facts

Description-Dependence and Social Relativity

Of the three constructivist theses before us, the most influential is the thesis of fact-constructivism— which is somewhat surprising given that it is also the most radical and the most counter-intuitive. Indeed, properly understood, fact-constructivism is such a bizarre view that it is hard to believe that anyone actually endorses it. And yet, it seems that many do.

According to fact-constructivism, it is a *necessary* truth about any fact that it obtains only because we humans have constructed it in a way that reflects our contingent needs and interests. This view stands opposed to fact-objectivism, according to which many facts about the world obtain entirely independently of human beings.

If we ask the fact-objectivist *which* facts obtain independently of us humans, he might volunteer some unsurprising examples: that there are mountains, that there were dinosaurs, that matter is made up of electrons. All of these, he might say, are examples of facts that are objective in the sense that they are fully mind-independent.

It is important to observe, however, that the fact-objectivist is not committed to *any* particular catalogue of mind-independent facts. All he is committed to is that there are *some* facts that obtain independently of us humans; he needn't claim, in addition, to *know* which facts those are. The fact-constructivist is not offering a different account of which facts obtain; nor is he claiming, as a radical skeptic might, that no one is in a position to *know* which facts obtain. The fact-constructivist need not disagree that the world contains facts about mountains, dinosaurs and electrons.

What the fact-constructivist is disputing is not our account of which facts there are, but a certain philosophical view of the *nature* of those facts, of what it is for there to be a fact of any sort in the first place. He thinks that, necessarily, no fact can obtain independently of societies and their contingent needs and interests.

Fact-constructivism would seem to run into an obvious problem. The world did not begin with us humans; many facts about it obtained before we did. How then could we have constructed them? For example, according to our best theory of the world, there were mountains on earth well before there were humans. How, then, could we be said to have constructed the fact that there are mountains on earth?

One famous constructivist, the French sociologist Bruno Latour, seems to have decided to just bite the bullet on this point. When French scientists working on the mummy of Ramses II (who died c. 1213 BC) concluded that Ramses probably died of tuberculosis, Latour denied that this was possible. "How could he pass away due to a bacillus discovered by Robert Koch in 1882?" Latour asked. Latour noted that just as it would be an anachronism to say that Ramses died from machine-gun fire so it would be an anachronism to say that he died of tuberculosis. As he boldly put it: "Before Koch, the bacillus had no real existence."[1]

[1] See Bruno Latour, "Ramses II est-il mort de la tuberculose?" La Recherche, 307 (March, 1998), 84–85. Quoted in Alan Sokal and Jean Bricmont, *Fashionable Nonsense: Postmodern Intellectuals' Abuse of Science* (New York: Picador Press, 1998), 96–7.

But this line is ill-advised for a fact-constructivist. Presumably, anyone must be able to make sense of the existence of facts which antedate the existence of human beings. A fact-constructivist is better off saying that even *those* facts—the facts that obtained before there were any human beings around to talk about them—were constructed by human beings. How to make sense of that is a very good question but for now I shall pretend that we can.

Let us turn instead to asking the following: How, according to the fact-constructivist, do we construct facts? How is the feat accomplished?

The most important and influential fact-constructivists in recent philosophy have been Nelson Goodman, Hilary Putnam and Richard Rorty. If we look at their writings, we see a fairly uniform answer to our question: we construct a fact by accepting a way of talking or thinking which describes that fact. Thus, Goodman, in his book *Ways of Worldmaking*, in a chapter entitled "The Fabrication of Facts," says:

... we make worlds by making versions ... [2]

where a "version," on Goodman's view, is in effect a set of descriptions of the world, very broadly understood.

And Rorty writes:

Take dinosaurs. Once you describe something as a dinosaur, its skin color and sex life are causally independent of your having so described it. But before you describe [something] as a dinosaur, or as anything else, there is no sense to the claim that it is "out there" having properties. [3]
... people like Goodman, Putnam and myself— ... think that there is no description-independent way the world is, no way it is under no description ... [4]

[2] Nelson Goodman, *Ways of Worldmaking* (Indianapolis: Hackett Publishing Co., 1978), 94.
[3] Richard Rorty, *Truth and Progress, Philosophical Papers, Volume 3* (New York: Cambridge University Press, 1998), 87.
[4] ibid. 90.

Let us call the view that Goodman and Rorty are gesturing at, the *Description Dependence of Facts*:

Necessarily, all facts are description-dependent: there cannot be a fact of the matter as to how things are with the world independently of our propensity to *describe* the world as being a certain way. Once we adopt a particular scheme for describing the world, there then come to be facts about the world.

This thesis is clearly a version of the view that all facts are mind-dependent since it is clearly only minds that are capable of describing the world. And as I have already emphasized, some facts are clearly description-dependent, or mind-dependent, in this sense. Nothing could be money, and no one could be a *priest* or a *president*, unless someone is—or at some point was—prepared so to describe them. The constructivist literature contains many other more controversial claims of the alleged description-dependence of facts. Michel Foucault, for example, famously argued that prior to the use of the concept **homosexual** to describe certain men there were no homosexuals but only men who preferred to have sex with other men.[5] I doubt Foucault's particular claim, but that is just to quibble about the definition of "homosexual." I do not doubt the general phenomenon.

But whatever one thinks about any particular case, the point is that it does not seem to be a *necessary truth* about *all* facts that they are in this way description- or mind-dependent. For example, facts about mountains, dinosaurs or electrons seem not to be description-dependent. Why should we think otherwise? What mistake in our ordinary, naïve realism about the world has the fact-constructivist uncovered? What positive reason is there to take such a prima facie counterintuitive view seriously?

It is not easy to find convincing answers to this question in the writings of the leading fact-constructivists.

[5] Michael Foucault, *The History of Sexuality, Volume 1: An Introduction*, trans. from the French by Robert Hurley (New York: Pantheon Books, 1978).

One problem which bedevils sensible discussion of this issue is that the radical thesis of fact-constructivism is often conflated with another thesis which, while itself not entirely uncontroversial, is nevertheless far less radical. As a result, fact-constructivism often appears to its proponents to be far less implausible than it actually is.

The thesis with which fact-constructivism is often conflated we may call the

Social Relativity of Descriptions:
Which scheme we adopt to describe the world will depend on which scheme we find it *useful* to adopt; and which scheme we find it useful to adopt will depend on our contingent needs and interests as social beings.

Rorty gives vivid expression to the social relativity of descriptions in the following passage:

... we describe giraffes as we do, *as* giraffes, because of our needs and interests. We speak a language which includes the word 'giraffe' because it suits our purposes to do so. The same goes for words like 'organ', 'cell,' 'atom' and so on—the names of the parts of things out of which giraffes are made so to speak. All the descriptions we give of things are suited to our purposes.... The line between a giraffe and the surrounding air is clear enough if you are a human being interested in hunting for meat. If you are a language-using ant or amoeba, or a space voyager describing us from above, that line is not so clear, and it is not so clear that you would need or have a word for 'giraffe' in your language.[6]

According to Rorty, we accept the descriptions we accept not because they "correspond to the way things are in and of themselves," but because it serves our practical interests to do so. Had we had different practical interests, we might well have

⁶ Richard Rorty, *Philosophy and Social Hope* (New York: Penguin, 1999), p. xxvi.

come to accept a very different set of descriptions of the world, ones which did not employ concepts—such as *giraffe* or *mountain*—with which we currently think.[7]

Rorty tries to justify his claim by inviting us to consider a hypothetical scenario in which we are non-meat-eating, language-using animals, more on the scale of an ant or an amoeba. Under those circumstances, he says, we may well not have had the concept *giraffe*.

Now, although I think that this thought experiment of Rorty's does not provide very good support for the social relativity of descriptions thesis—his thought experiment varies not only our practical interests but our biological and physical properties as well—I propose for the purposes of the present chapter simply to grant him that thesis (we shall discuss a closely related view in Chapter 8). For now, my main concern is to emphasize that the social relativity of descriptions thesis is entirely independent of the thesis of the description-dependence of facts, and lends it no support whatsoever.

Rorty and others often suggest otherwise. For example, immediately after he says—

The line between a giraffe and the surrounding air is clear enough if you are a human being interested in hunting for meat. If you are a language-using ant or amoeba, or a space voyager describing us from above, that line is not so clear, and it is not so clear that you would need or have a word for 'giraffe' in your language.

—Rorty goes on to say:

More generally, it is not clear that any of the millions of ways of describing the bit of space time occupied by what we call a giraffe is closer to the way things are in and of themselves than any of the others.[8]

[7] Rorty goes back and forth between talking about having the concept *giraffe* and having the word 'giraffe' in one's language; these are different ideas, but the difference won't matter for our purposes here.

[8] ibid.

But it is simply not true that a denial of description-independent facts is a *generalization* of the social relativity of descriptions.

It is one thing to say that we must explain our acceptance of certain descriptions in terms of our practical interest rather than in terms of their correspondence to the way things are in and of themselves; and it's quite another to say that there is no such thing as a way things are in and of themselves, independently of our descriptions. It is entirely possible to hold the former thesis without in any way endorsing the latter.

To see this clearly, we need to emphasize that even the most extreme fact-objectivist will want to admit that there can be many equally true descriptions of the world at any given moment in time, including some that may well strike us as quite bizarre. Imagine, for example, a giraffe chewing on a eucalyptus tree, and suppose that that tree is located roughly three miles from where the Emperor Nero happens to be at that moment. It would then be correct to describe the giraffe as a giraffe, but also as an object that is less than four miles from an emperor.

To concede the social relativity of descriptions is to agree that which of these descriptions will strike us as "worth having" will depend on our practical interests. I have suggested conceding this claim for the moment. It is certainly true that some of these descriptions will strike us as more useful than others in ways that will depend on our interests. Since all sorts of things could be less than four miles from an emperor, knowing only that something satisfies that description will not tell us anything about what it is likely to do. On the other hand, knowing that something satisfies the concept *giraffe* can tell us a quite a lot: that the animal in question has a long neck, that it feeds on the leaves of acacia trees, that it has a heart and lungs, and so forth.

However, it clearly doesn't *follow* from any of this that no description of the world could be any closer to the way things are in and of themselves than any other. For all that the social relativity of descriptions allows us to say, if I were to call the chunk of space-time occupied by the giraffe a tree, or a mountain, or a dinosaur or an asteroid—all of those descriptions would simply be false by virtue of not corresponding to the way things are.

The social relativity of descriptions is one thing and fact-constructivism is another. Fact-constructivism depends on the claim, which the social relativity of descriptions does nothing to support, that we can only make sense of there being a fact of the matter about the world after we have agreed to employ some descriptions of it as opposed to others, that prior to the use of those descriptions, there can be no sense to the idea that there is a fact of the matter 'out there' constraining which of our descriptions are true and which false.

Why should we believe this radical and counterintuitive claim?

Arguing for the Description-Dependence of Facts

Nelson Goodman has attempted to tell us why. He begins by reflecting on the notion of a *constellation*.

About the "Big Dipper," he writes:

Has a constellation been there as long as the stars that compose it, or did it come into being when selected and designated? ... And what could be meant by saying that the constellation was always there, before any version? Does this mean that all configurations of stars whatever are always constellations whether or not picked out and designated as such? I suggest that to say that all configurations are constellations is in effect to say that none are: that a constellation becomes such only through being chosen from among all configurations, much as a class becomes a kind only through being distinguished, according to some principle, from other classes.[9]

9 Nelson Goodman, "Notes on the Well-Made World," in *Starmaking: Realism, Anti-Realism, and Irrealism,* ed. Peter McCormick (Cambridge, Mass.: The MIT Press, 1996), 156.

Let's set aside for now ontological questions regarding the stars that compose the Big Dipper, worrying only about the constellation that they compose. Should we say that the Big Dipper existed prior to our having selected it for special attention, or should we say, rather, that it is the very act of selecting that particular configuration of stars that made them into the constellation the Big Dipper?

Goodman recoils from the thought that the Big Dipper was sitting out there waiting to be noticed and named. For if we take the Big Dipper to have existed prior to our naming, he says, we would have to say that all possible configurations of stars, including the innumerable many that we have not chosen to single out for special attention, count as constellations. And this he regards as absurd. So, at least in the case of facts about which groups of stars constitute constellations, our describing them as so is essential to their being so.

Having thus established that constellations are description-dependent, Goodman proceeds to generalize the view to all facts:

Now as we thus make constellations by picking out and putting together certain stars rather than others, so we make stars by drawing certain boundaries rather than others. Nothing dictates whether the skies shall be marked off into constellations or other objects. We have to make what we find, be it the Great Dipper, Sirius, food, fuel, or a stereo system.[10]

This, however, is not a terribly promising line of argument.

To begin with, "constellation" looks to be one of those words, like "priest" or "president," that is obviously description-dependent. Most dictionaries define "constellation" in something like the way the *American Heritage College Dictionary* does, as "an arbitrary formation of stars perceived as a figure or design, esp. one of 88 recognized groups." As this definition indicates, then, it

[10] Ibid.

is part of the very concept of a constellation that it is a configuration of stars that has been noticed by human perceivers on Earth to form a distinctive shape.

It follows trivially from such a definition that the Big Dipper did not exist prior to its being noticed and named, for to be a constellation, on this definition, is precisely to be a group of stars that has been noticed and named. As a result, we could not say that every possible configuration of stars counts as a constellation, for not every possible configuration will trace a distinctive figure when viewed from Earth by creatures like us.

On this standard understanding of constellation, then, it is simply a trivial fact about constellations that they exist only if they have been noticed by human perceivers: that is simply part of their definition. As a result, no argument based on them could possibly hope to sustain the generalized constructivism about facts that Goodman is after.

But there is an even more fundamental problem with Goodman's argument for a generalized description-dependence of facts and that is that his own model of description-dependence appears to require that some facts *not* be description-dependent. Let me explain.

Goodman's picture seems to be something like this: we construct facts by using concepts to group some things together. Our concepts work like cookie cutters: they carve the world up into facts by drawing boundaries one way rather than another. We take a certain collection of stars, draw lines between them, and call them a constellation and that is how there come to be constellations; we take a certain collection of molecules, draw a line around them, and call them a star and that is how there come to be stars.

Now, if that is to be a general account of how facts are constructed we had better be able to extend it all the way down, to the level of the most basic facts. So let us iterate Goodman's picture a few more times. We take a certain collection of atoms, draw a line around them, and call them a molecule and that is how there come to be molecules. We take a certain collection of electrons, protons and neutrons, draw a line around them, and call them an atom and that is how there come to be atoms. And so forth.

There need be no suggestion, on this picture, that we lack *reasons* to draw these lines in the way that we do. But these reasons are *pragmatic*, through and through: it serves our practical purposes to carve up the world one way rather than another. The crucial point, for Goodman's purposes is that none of these ways of carving up the world can be said to be any closer to the way things are in and of themselves than any other way, for there is no way things are in and of themselves.

If, however, this is our picture of how facts are constructed, won't we at some point come across some stuff whose properties are not determined in this way? If our concepts are cutting lines into some basic worldly dough and thus imbuing it with a structure it would not otherwise possess, doesn't there have to be some worldly dough for them to get to work on, and mustn't the basic properties of that dough be determined independently of all of this fact-constituting activity? This basic dough can be quite spare. Perhaps it is just the space-time manifold, or a distribution of energy, or whatever. Still, must there not be some such basic stuff for this picture even to make sense? And if there is, doesn't that put paid to a generalized description-dependence of facts?

We can illustrate the point here by looking at another famous argument for the description-dependence of facts, this one due to Hilary Putnam.[11]

Putnam invites us to consider a world with "three individuals" in it, which we can represent as shown in Figure 3.1:

[11] Cf. John Searle, *The Construction of Social Reality* (New York: The Free Press, 1995), 165–6.

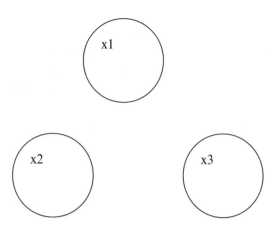

How many objects does this little world contain?

On a commonsensical notion of "object," there are exactly three objects in this world, x_1, x_2 and x_3. However, Putnam observes,

Suppose ... like some Polish logicians, I believe that for every two particulars there is an object which is their sum .... [then] I will find that the world of "three individuals" ... actually contains *seven* objects.[12]

The lesson, Putnam says, is that there is no fact of the matter how many objects there are in this world. If you pick the conceptual scheme employed by common sense, you will say that there are three objects, x_1, x_2, x_3; however, if you pick the scheme employed by certain Polish logicians, you will say that there are seven objects, namely, x_1, x_2, x_3, $x_1 + x_2$, $x_1 + x_3$, $x_2 + x_3$, $x_1 + x_2 + x_3$. On the basis of this little argument, Putnam concludes that it is nonsense to think that there is a way things are in and of themselves, independently of the selection of a conceptual scheme.

[12] Hilary Putnam, *Realism with a Human Face* (Cambridge, Mass.: Harvard University Press), 96.

This, however, is a mistake. All that Putnam's example shows is that there can be many equally true descriptions of the world, or of a certain portion of it. And as we have already seen, no fact-objectivist would deny that. Any fact-objectivist would accept that, for any given chunk of space-time, there can be many equally true descriptions of it, provided they are all consistent with one another. All that he is committed to is that *not every possible* description of a given chunk of space-time will be true, that some such descriptions will be false by virtue of not corresponding to what is there.

But isn't Putnam's little world a counterexample to fact-objectivism, even as so understood? For aren't the descriptions that we are allowed to give of it—three objects versus seven objects—inconsistent with each other? Surely, it can't both be the case that there are exactly three objects in the world and that there are exactly seven!

The answer, of course, is that these descriptions are perfectly consistent with each other, because they involve entirely distinct notions of "object." They no more contradict each other than my saying that there are eight people at the party contradicts my saying that there are four couples at that very same party.

So Putnam's example fails to prove description-dependence. Indeed, it actually lends support to its negation.

The point is that, for any such example to work, we need to start with some basic facts—for example, that there are three circles—that we can then truthfully redescribe in a variety of different ways. Given that the little world contains three circles, we can then introduce a notion of "object" on which it is true to say that there are three objects, and a different notion of "object" on which it is true to say that there are seven objects or nine objects or whatever.

But for this sort of strategy of redescription to make sense, it must be assumed that there are some basic facts—the basic worldly dough—on which our redescriptive strategies can get to work. But that is precisely what fact-constructivism denies.

Fact-Constructivism: Three Problems

We can search far and wide for better or more convincing arguments for description-dependence; but we would come up empty. As far as I can tell, once one distinguishes carefully between the description-dependence of facts and the social relativity of descriptions, fact-constructivists have very little to offer us beyond the sorts of unpersuasive examples deployed by Goodman and Putnam.

So far, I have been arguing that we have been given no good argument for believing that all facts are description-dependent, and thus no reason for doubting the common-sense view that many facts about the world are independent of us. Quite the contrary, we have seen reason to think that fact-objectivism is presupposed even by the sort of cookie-cutter constructivism with which Goodman seeks to oppose it.

But the case against fact-constructivism is stronger than this. It's not merely that we have been given no reason to take the view seriously; it's that we can give seemingly decisive reasons against its ultimate coherence. There are at least three serious problems.

First, and as I mentioned at the beginning of this chapter, it's a truism about most of the objects and facts that we talk about—electrons, mountains, dinosaurs, giraffes, rivers and lakes—that their existence *antedates* ours. How, then, could their existence depend on us? How could we create our own past? Wouldn't this commit us to a bizarre form of backwards causation, where the cause (our activity) comes later than its effect (the existence of the dinosaurs)? Let us call this the problem of *causation*.

Second, and even if we did suppose that the universe has existed only for as long as we have, isn't it part of the very *concept* of an electron, or of a mountain, that these things were *not* constructed by us? Take electrons, for example. Is it not part of the very purpose of having such a concept that it is to designate things that are independent of us? According to the Standard Model of particle physics, electrons are among the fundamental building blocks of all matter. They constitute the ordinary macroscopic objects that we see and with which we interact, including our own bodies. How, then, could their existence depend on us? If we insist on saying that they were constructed by our descriptions of them, don't we run the risk of saying something not merely false but *conceptually incoherent*, as if we hadn't quite grasped what an electron was supposed to be? Let us call this the problem of *conceptual competence*.

Finally, and perhaps most decisively, there is what we may call *the problem of disagreement*.

As I pointed out in the last chapter, it is in principle possible to combine a constructivism about a given fact P with the view that we were somehow metaphysically constrained to construct P, once we had considered the question. But as I also pointed out, the social constructivist is not interested in such mandated constructions. His whole point is to emphasize the dependence of any fact on our *contingent* social needs and interests, so that if our needs and interests had been different then so, too, would have been the relevant facts.

And it is just as well that the social constructivist rejects mandated constructions, for it is in fact very hard to make sense of them. If a given fact really does owe its existence to our intentional activities, it is hard to see how there could fail to be *possible* circumstances in which we might have chosen to construct a different fact incompatible with it. (Kant's own claim about geometry came to grief: soon after he made it, Riemann discovered non-Euclidean geometries, and some one hundred years later, Einstein showed that physical space was in fact non-Euclidean.)

Suppose, then, to put the matter in general schematic terms, that we construct the fact that P, and that the construction in question is metaphysically contingent. Then it follows that it is possible that some *other* society should have constructed the fact that not-P, even while we construct the fact that P.

So far, so good, for that is precisely what the constructivist is after. However, we are now able to argue as follows.

1. Since we have constructed the fact that P, P.
2. And since it is possible that another community should have constructed the fact that not-P, then possibly not-P.
3. So: It is possible that both P and not-P.

But how could one and the same world be such that, in it, it is possibly the case both that P and that not-P? How could it be the case both that the first Americans originated in Asia *and* that they did not originate there but originated instead in a subterranean world of spirits? How could it be the case both that the world is flat (the fact constructed by pre-Aristotelian Greeks) *and* that it is round (the fact constructed by us)? And so forth.[13]

Social constructivism about facts looks to be in direct violation of the Law of Non-Contradiction:

Non-Contradiction:

Necessarily: It is not the case both that P and that not-P.

The problem doesn't depend on there *actually* being two communities that have constructed mutually incompatible facts. So long as it is simply *possible* that one community has constructed P and that another has constructed either the fact that not-P, or a fact Q that entails that not-P, we get a violation of non-contradiction.

[13] A version of the problem of disagreement is discussed by André Kukla, *Social Constructivism and the Philosophy of Science* (London and New York: Routledge, 2000), 91–104.

This problem of disagreement is a perfectly general problem for a constructivism about any domain; the problem doesn't just arise for a global constructivist thesis. So long as the constructions are said to be contingent, there will be a problem about how we are to accommodate the possible simultaneous construction of logically (or metaphysically) incompatible facts.

It is impossible, I believe, to see how the thesis of description-dependence, construed in the manner of Goodman's cookie-cutter constructivism, could have an adequate answer to these three problems. Against that view, these objections are decisive.

Richard Rorty, however, has long complained that description-dependence is not best implemented by cookie-cutter constructivism, but rather by a different understanding of how facts depend on our descriptive activities. His view, as we shall see, is tailor-made to get around the three problems we have just raised for constructivism. We shall examine Rorty's distinctive brand of constructivism in the next chapter.

4

Relativizing the Facts

Rorty's Relativistic Constructivism

WITH special reference to the problem of conceptual competence, Rorty writes:

... people like Goodman, Putnam and myself—people who think that there is no description-independent way the world is, no way it is under no description—keep being tempted to use Kantian form-matter metaphors. We are tempted to say that there were no objects before language shaped the raw material (a lot of ding-an-sichy, all content-and-no-scheme stuff). But as soon as we say anything like this we find ourselves accused (plausibly) of making the false causal claim that the invention of "dinosaur" caused dinosaurs to come into existence—of being what our opponents call "linguistic idealists."[1]

If, however, we are not to understand the construction of facts on this Kantian cookie-cutter model, according to which our concepts cut boundaries into the "raw material" of the world, thereby causing there to be such things as dinosaurs, how then are we to understand it?

---

[1] Rorty, *Truth and Progress*, 90.

Here is what Rorty has to say (it will prove useful to quote him at some length):

... none of us antirepresentationalists have ever doubted that most things in the universe are causally independent of us. What we question is whether they are representationally independent of us. For X to be representationally independent of us is for X to have an intrinsic feature (a feature that it has under any and every description) such that it is better described by some of our terms rather than others. Because we can see no way of deciding which descriptions of an object get at what is "intrinsic" to it, as opposed to merely its "relational," extrinsic features (e.g., its description-relative features), we are prepared to discard the intrinsic-extrinsic distinction, the claim that beliefs represent, and the whole question of representational independence or dependence. This means discarding the idea of (as Bernard Williams has put it) "how things are *anyway*," apart from whether or how they are described.

[My critics seem] to think that neither I nor anyone else would feel any "serious temptation to deny that the claim ... 'There are no chairs in this room' will be true or false in virtue of the way things are, or the nature of reality." But I do in fact feel tempted to deny this. I do so because I see two ways of interpreting "in virtue of the way things are." One is short for "in virtue of the way our current descriptions of things are used and the causal interactions we have with those things." The other is short for "*simply* in virtue of the way things are, quite apart from how we describe them." On the first interpretation, I think that true propositions about the presence of chairs, the existence of neutrinos, the desirability of respect for the dignity of our fellow beings, *and everything else* are true "in virtue of the way things are." On the second interpretation, I think that *no* proposition is true "in virtue of the way things are."[2]

Although it is not easy to make sense of everything in this passage, the basic idea seems to be this.[3] On the cookie-cutter

2 Ibid. 86–7.
3 Rorty exegesis is a notoriously tricky matter. So think of me as making the following claim: if there is anything in Rorty's writings which will help the fact-constructivist with the problems we have uncovered, it is the view I am attributing to him.

model, we literally make it the case that certain facts obtain—that there are giraffes, for example—by describing the world in terms of the concept **giraffe**. But this is to buy in on the Kantian play with form and content and to court the problems about the relation between mind and reality outlined above.

The right way to think about the matter, rather, is to regard all talk about facts as just so much talk about how things are according to some theory of the world—or "language game," as Rorty sometimes puts it, using Wittgenstein's metaphor. No sense can be made of the idea that reality is a certain way in and of itself. And no sense can be made of the idea that the mind causes the world to be a certain way, through its use of descriptions. The only notion we can make sense of is that of the world's being a certain way *according* to some way of talking about it, *relative* to some theory of it.[4]

Now, we need to understand better this idea of a proposition's being true only relative to a theory, and not just true simpliciter, and we shall turn to that in a moment. But I think we are already in a position to see that, if Rorty's idea were cogent, it would help significantly with the three problems we outlined for fact-constructivism.

Suppose we may never claim that some propositions are simply true but only that they are true relative to this or that way of talking. The ways of talking themselves can't be said to be truer than one another, or more faithful to the way things are in and of themselves than one another, because there is no way things are in and of themselves. There is just one way of talking as opposed to another.

---

[4] Ian Hacking seems to have a similar idea in mind when he writes: "The world is so autonomous, so much to itself, that it does not even have what we call structure in itself. We make our puny representations of the world, but all the structure of which we can conceive lies within our representations." Hacking, *The Social Construction of What?*, 85.

Does that imply that one can talk anyway one pleases, that there are no constraints on which descriptions of the world to adopt? Well, yes and no. Reality as it is in itself won't stand in the way of our talking one way as opposed to another, since there is no such thing as reality as it is in itself.

As Rorty explains, however, that does not mean that all ways of talking will be on a par; we will prefer some ways of talking to others, for pragmatic reasons. We will prefer some ways of talking to others because some of these ways will prove more *useful* to us in satisfying our needs. In ordinary life, when we simply claim something to be true, what we mean (or anyway ought to mean) is that it is true relative to *our* preferred way of talking, a way of talking that we will have adopted because it has come to seem so useful to us.

Now, notice that according to our way of talking, most aspects of the world are causally independent of us and antedate our existence. As Rorty puts it:

Given that it pays to talk about mountains, as it certainly does, one of the obvious truths about mountains is that they were here before we talked about them. If you do not believe that, you probably do not know how to play the language games that employ the word "mountain." But the utility of those language games has nothing to do with the question of whether Reality as It Is In Itself, apart from the way in which it is handy for human beings to describe it, has mountains in it.[5]

It is, therefore, correct, on Rorty's view, to say that we do not make the mountains and that they existed before we did; those are claims that are licensed by a way of talking that we have adopted. However, that does not mean that it is just plain true that there are mountains independently of humans; it never makes sense to say that anything is just plain true. All we can

[5] Richard Rorty, "Does Academic Freedom have Philosophical Presuppositions: Academic Freedom and the Future of the University," *Academe* 80, no. 6 (November–December 1994), 57.

intelligibly talk about is what is true according to this or that way of talking, some of which it pays for us to adopt. That takes care of the problems of causation and conceptual competence.

It might help to understand Rorty's view here, by thinking of it on analogy with what we would say about truth in a fiction. We all know that the characters in a novel are constructions of the author. But within the novel, the characters are not thought of as being constructed (except possibly by their parents). They are thought of, rather, as real people, with real biological origins. Thus, it is true according to the fiction *The Amazing Adventures of Kavalier and Clay,* that Joseph Kavalier was a Jew who fled from Nazi-occupied Prague, and that his parents died at the hands of the Nazis.[6]

Similarly, the Rortian constructivist thinks that once we decide upon a given theory of the world that includes the description "There are mountains" (as the author decides upon his various characters), it is true according to that theory that mountains are causally independent of us, and that they existed before we did.

Rorty's relativistic constructivism also provides a smooth solution to the problem of disagreement. Just as it can be true according to one fiction that P and true according to another fiction that not-P, so there is no difficulty accommodating the fact that it may pay for one community to, for example, affirm the existence of immaterial souls and pay for another community to reject them. Since

It's true according to C1's theory T1, that there are X's

in no way contradicts

It's true according to C2's theory T2, that there are no X's,

---

[6] Michael Chabon, *The Amazing Adventures of Kavalier and Clay* (New York: Picador USA, 2000). For the suggestion that this analogy might be helpful in explaining Rorty's view, I am grateful to Nishiten Shah.

the views are not in competition with each other and the problem of disagreement simply disappears.

Going relativistic, then, seems to help with all three of the seemingly insuperable problems we uncovered for fact-constructivism in the previous chapter. And it is hard to see what else could help. If fact-constructivism is to work at all, then, it looks as though it *has* to assume this relativistic Rortian form.

In particular, it looks as though there can be no solution to the problem of disagreement without resorting to relativization. This is a general lesson for constructivist views, even for those, unlike the one currently under discussion, which are restricted to local domains and are not meant to apply to all facts.

Take any unrelativized proposition P and any community C. So long as the constructions in question are metaphysically contingent, there can be no question of our saying that C constructed the fact that P. Any such view would immediately violate the principle of non-contradiction. Rather, the most that any such constructivist view will be able to say is that C constructs the relativized fact:

According to C: P

or something along similar lines.

Contemporary would-be constructivists, it seems to me, even those working within the analytic tradition, have paid insufficient attention to this point.[7]

Relativisms Local and Global

Rorty's postmodernist brand of global relativism harks back to Protagoras' famous pronouncement: "Man is the measure of all

[7] For an example of a contemporary constructivism about morality see Christine Korsgaard, *The Sources of Normativity* (Cambridge: Cambridge University Press, 1996).

things."[8] Historically, though, the most influential relativistic theses have been directed at *specific* domains, at truth in *morality*, for example, or *aesthetics*, or *etiquette*. It will prove useful to pause for a bit and examine how we should construe them.[9]

Take the important case of morality. Imagine Eliot uttering the sentence:

1. "It was wrong of Ken to steal that money"

The moral relativist begins with the observation there are no facts in the world which could make such an absolute judgment true. No act is ever simply morally right or morally wrong. Let us put this by saying that a moral relativist begins by endorsing the thesis of *moral non-absolutism:*

Moral Non-Absolutism:

2. There are no absolute moral facts which can confirm absolute moral judgments.

Now, any thinker who endorses moral non-absolutism faces a choice. He must say what he proposes to do about our ordinary moral utterances, given that he has come to endorse a view about them which implies that all such utterances are uniformly false.

The response of the moral nihilist is to advocate abandoning moral discourse altogether. His view is that the discovery that there are no absolute facts of the required kind renders the

[8] By "global" I mean "inclusive of all subject matters," rather than "applying everywhere on the globe."

[9] I will develop one especially influential way of formulating a relativistic view of a particular domain—an approach I will call "thoroughgoing relativism." It begins with, but somewhat modifies, Gilbert Harman's fine discussion of moral relativism in his contribution to Harman and Thomson, *Moral Relativism and Moral Objectivity.* There are at least two other approaches to the formulation of local relativism in the literature. One—which starts from the idea that a relativistic view of a given domain consists in the claim that in that domain we can have true contradictions—I regard as hopeless. Another approach, which I call "absolutist relativism," I will discuss briefly in Chapter 6.

discourse of morality useless, in much the way that one might think that the putative discovery that there is no God renders religious discourse irremediably useless.

The moral expressivist, on the other hand, attempts to hang onto moral discourse by attempting to construe moral utterances so that they are taken to express not judgments but rather the speaker's affective states of mind. Thus, a moral emotivist will construe Eliot's saying

"It was wrong of Ken to steal that money"

as saying roughly:

3. Boo, to Ken's stealing that money!

Since saying Boo! to someone's doing something is not to say anything that could be either true or false, it no longer matters that there are no facts to validate the truth of moral utterances.

The moral relativist disagrees both with the moral nihilist and with the moral expressivist. By contrast with the moral nihilist, the moral relativist advocates retaining moral discourse; and by contrast with the moral expressivist, he advocates retaining the appearance that moral utterances express truth-apt judgments. His solution is to recommend that we so construe moral utterances that they report not on the sorts of absolute fact that have been conceded not to obtain, but on the sorts of *relational* fact that no one disputes. A reasonable first stab at formulating the relativist's recommendation might look something like this:

Moral Relationism (first stab):
If Eliot's moral judgment is to have any prospect of being true, we must not construe his utterance of

"It was wrong of Ken to steal that money"

as expressing the claim

It was wrong of Ken to steal that money,

but rather as expressing the claim:

4. *According to moral framework M, it was wrong of Ken to steal that money.*

This reasonable first stab must soon give way to a small but important modification. The point is that in making his utterance, Eliot was *endorsing* a view about Ken's stealing that money, whereas a merely relational judgment like (4) is just a logical statement about the relation between the moral framework M and the judgment that it was wrong of Ken to steal that money. Even someone who disagreed with Eliot that it was wrong of Ken to steal that money could agree with (4).

To see that, consider George. George is not inclined to say that it was wrong of Ken to steal that money because George does not accept moral code M but rather a different moral code, M*, according to which it was not wrong of Ken to steal that money. Still, George could agree that, *according to M*, it was wrong of Ken to steal that money.

To accommodate this point, then, we must modify the relationist clause so that it makes reference to the speaker's *acceptance* of the particular moral framework to which he must, according to relativism, relativize his moral claims, thus:

Moral Relationism:
If Eliot's moral judgment is to have any prospect of being true, we must not construe his utterance of

"It was wrong of Ken to steal that money"

as expressing the claim

It was wrong of Ken to steal that money,
but rather as expressing the claim:

5. *According to moral framework M, that I, Eliot, accept, it was wrong of Ken to steal that money.*

Finally, in order to emphasize that there is nothing that privileges any one of these moral frameworks over any of the others, the relativist typically adds a clause saying as much:

Moral Pluralism:
There are many alternative moral frameworks, but no facts by virtue of which one of them is more correct than any of the others.

Moral relativism, then, is the combination of moral non-absolutism, moral relationism and moral pluralism, all three theses now suitably generalized.

Moral Relativism

6. There are no absolute moral facts which can confirm absolute moral judgments.

7. If S's moral judgments are to have any prospect of being true, we must not construe his utterances of the form

   "It is wrong of P to A"

as expressing the claim

   It is wrong of P to A,

but rather as expressing the claim:

According to moral framework M, that I, S, accept, it is wrong of P to A

8. There are many alternative moral frameworks, but no facts by virtue of which one of them is more correct than any of the others.

Now, Rorty's global relativism is an attempt to generalize such a relativistic conception to *all* domains. As he puts it, there are many alternative schemes for describing the world, none of which can be said to be more faithful to the way things are in and of themselves, for there is no way things are in and of themselves.

Of course, some of these theories will be more useful to us than others, and so we will accept some but not others. Those that we accept will naturally be more salient to us as we make claims about the world. So we go around saying

"There are giraffes"

not

"There are giraffes according to a theory that we accept."

Nevertheless, it is not, and cannot, *simply* be true that there are giraffes (just as Rorty says that it cannot *simply* be true that there are chairs in this room); at best what's true is that there are giraffes according to a way of talking that we find it useful to accept.

Global Relativism about Facts:
   9. There are no absolute facts of the form, p.
  10. If our factual judgments are to have any prospect of being true, we must not construe utterances of the form

      "p"

      as expressing the claim

      p

      but rather as expressing the claim

      According to a theory, T, that we accept, p.

  11. There are many alternative theories for describing the world, but no facts by virtue of which one is more faithful to the way things are in and of themselves than any of the others.

Rejecting Global Relativism: The Traditional Argument

Philosophers have long suspected that a global relativism about facts is a fundamentally incoherent position. A local relativism about a specific domain—moral relativism, for example—may not be particularly plausible; but it seems coherent. In contrast, many philosophers have held that a relativism gone global makes no sense. Why not?

The rough idea behind this oft-repeated traditional objection is that *any* relativistic thesis needs to commit itself to there being at least *some* absolute truths; yet what a global relativism asserts is that there are *no* absolute truths. Hence, a global relativism is bound to be incoherent.

I agree with this traditional objection—though I do not agree with the traditional argument by which it is defended.

The traditional argument is elegantly rendered by Thomas Nagel (Nagel uses the words "subjective" and "objective" in place of my "relative" and absolute," respectively):

...the claim "Everything is subjective" must be nonsense, for it would itself have to be either subjective or objective. But it can't be objective, since in that case it would be false if true. And it can't be subjective, because then it would not rule out any objective claim, including the claim that it is objectively false. There may be some subjectivists, perhaps styling themselves as pragmatists, who present subjectivism as applying even to itself. But then it does not call for a reply, since it is a report of what the subjectivist finds it agreeable to say. If he also invites us to join him, we need not offer any reason for declining since he has offered us no reason to accept.[10]

According to this traditional argument, then, the global relativist is caught on the horns of a dilemma. Either he intends his own view to be absolutely true, or he intends it to be only relatively true, true relative to some theory or other. If the former, he refutes himself, for he would then have admitted at least one absolute truth. If the latter, we may just ignore him, for then it is just a report of what the relativist finds it agreeable to say.

Relativists are prone to dismissing self-refutation arguments of this sort as clever bits of logical trickery that have no real bearing on the issues at hand. That attitude, I think, is a mistake. It is always a good idea to ask how some very general view about truth, knowledge, or meaning applies to itself; and few things

[10] Thomas Nagel, *The Last Word* (Oxford: Oxford University Press, 1997), 15.

could be more damaging to a view than to discover that it is false *by its own lights*. Having said that, however, it has to be noted that it is not clear that this particular self-refutation argument is sound, for it is not clear that it follows from the concession that relativism is itself to be true only relative to a theory, that it is just a report of what the relativist "finds it agreeable to say." Perhaps relativism is true relative to a theory that it pays for us all to accept, relativists and non-relativists alike.

For this reason, then, I am not impressed with the traditional argument for the claim that global relativism is self-refuting. There is, however, a stronger argument to the same effect.

Rejecting Global Relativism: A Different Argument

The global relativist maintains that there could be no facts of the form

12. There have been dinosaurs

but only facts of the form

13. According to a theory that we accept, there have been dinosaurs.

Well and good. But are we now supposed to think that there are absolute facts of this latter form, facts about which theories we accept?

There are three problems for the relativist who answers "yes" to this question. First, and most decisively, he would be abandoning any hope of expressing the view he wanted to express, namely that there are no absolute facts of any kind, but only relative facts. Instead, he would end up expressing the view that the only absolute facts there are, are facts about what theories different communities accept. He would be proposing, in other words, that the only absolute facts there are, are facts about our *beliefs*. And this would no longer be a global relativism.

Second, this would be a very peculiar view in its own right, for it's hard to believe that there is a difficulty about absolute facts concerning mountains and giraffes, but none concerning what beliefs people have. This seems to get things exactly the wrong way round. It is the mental that has always seemed most puzzling to philosophers, not the physical—so much so, indeed, that many of them have been driven to rejecting facts about the mental outright, eliminating them from their conception of what the world contains. Philosophers who advocate doing this are called "eliminativists," and it is perhaps just a little ironic that one of the most influential early eliminativists was Richard Rorty himself.[11]

Finally, the relativist is not driven to his position by the peculiar thought that facts about the mental are somehow in better shape than facts about the physical; if that were his motivation, he would owe us a very different sort of argument from the one to which he typically appeals. It would have to be an argument not about the mysteriousness of absolute facts as such, but about the mysteriousness of absolute facts about the physical in particular, in contrast with those concerning the mental. But that is not at all what the global relativist has in mind. His initial thought, rather, is that there is something incoherent about the very possibility of an absolute fact, whether this concerns physical facts or mental facts or normative facts.

It is, therefore, not really a viable option for the relativist to answer "yes" to the question we posed: are there absolute facts of the kind described in (13)? But what would it mean to answer "no"?

If it isn't simply true that we accept a theory according to which there have been dinosaurs, then that must be because that

---

[11] See, for instance, Richard Rorty, "Mind-Body Identity, Privacy, and Categories," *Review of Metaphysics* 19 (1965): 24–54.

fact itself obtains only relative to a theory that we accept. So, the thought must be that the only facts there are, are of the form:

> According to a theory that we accept, there is a theory that we accept and according to this latter theory, there have been dinosaurs.

And, now, of course, the dialectic repeats itself. At each stage of the looming regress, the relativist will have to deny that the claim at that stage can be simply true and will have to insist that it itself is true only relative to a theory that we accept.

The upshot is that the fact-relativist is committed to the view that the only facts there are, are infinitary facts of the form:

> According to a theory that we accept, there is a theory that we accept and according to this latter theory, there is a theory that we accept and ... there have been dinosaurs.

But it is absurd to propose that, in order for our utterances to have any prospect of being true, what we must mean by them are infinitary propositions that we could neither express nor understand.

The real dilemma facing the global relativist, then, is this: either the formulation that he offers us does not succeed in expressing the view that there are only relative facts; or it consists in the claim that we should so reinterpret our utterances that they express infinitary propositions that we can neither express nor understand.

In a sense, this difficulty should have been obvious from the start. Our grip on relativistic views derives from our grip on local relativisms—relativistic views of such specific domains as the polite and the moral. Local relativisms, however, explicitly commit themselves to the existence of absolute truths: what they claim is that judgments in a given domain have to be relativized to a parameter if they are to have absolute truth conditions. Once they are so relativized, though, they then *do* have absolute truth conditions and so are capable of absolute truth or falsity. As a result, they do not offer us a model for how we might escape commitment to absolute truth as such.

Conclusion

There are two ways to try to implement the thought that all facts are constructed: cookie-cutter constructivism and relativistic constructivism. Both versions face decisive difficulties. The cookie-cutter version succumbs to the problems with causation, conceptual competence and disagreement. And the relativistic version faces a decisive dilemma: either it isn't intelligible or it isn't relativism.

We have no choice but to recognize that there must be some objective, mind-independent facts.

This argument, of course, doesn't tell us all by itself which facts obtain and which ones don't; nor does it tell us, of the facts that do obtain, which ones are mind-independent and which ones aren't.

But once we see that there is no general philosophical obstacle to acknowledging mind-independent facts, we also see that we have been given no reason for supposing that those facts aren't just the ones we always took them to be—facts about dinosaurs, giraffes, mountains, and so forth.

5

Epistemic Relativism Defended

Introduction

IF the argument of the previous two chapters is correct, we have no choice but to think that the world out there is what it is largely independently of us and our beliefs about it. There are many facts that we did not have a hand in shaping. If we want to have a true conception of the way the world is, our beliefs need to accurately reflect those mind-independent facts.

Of course, the world doesn't just inscribe itself onto our minds. In trying to get at the truth, what we do is try to figure out what's true from the evidence available to us: we try to form the belief that it would be most *rational* to have, given the evidence.

But is there just *one* way of forming rational beliefs in response to the evidence? Are facts about justification universal or might they vary from community to community?

Just as there are moral relativists who think that there are no universal moral facts, so there are *epistemic relativists* who think that there are no universal epistemic facts, that facts about what belief is justified by a given item of evidence can vary from community to community. If these latter philosophers are right, then different people may rationally arrive at opposed conclusions, even as they acknowledge all the same data; or so it would appear.

A proponent of equal validity, then, can easily agree with our negative assessment of fact-constructivism, for he can hope to make good on a constructivist view of rational belief. He can forego the idea that *all* facts vary from social context to social context while maintaining the much weaker thesis that facts about rational belief do.

Just as before, of course, a constructivist view of rational belief had better assume an explicitly relativistic form, if it is to avoid the problem of disagreement; and I shall henceforth assume that it does. As we shall see, in contrast with the case of fact-constructivism, there looks to be a powerful argument in support of a relativistic view of rational belief.

Once again, we turn to Richard Rorty for the most vivid exposition of the view. But first, some potted astronomical history.

Rorty on Cardinal Bellarmine

Up until the sixteenth century, the dominant view of the universe was that it was a closed space, bounded by a spherical envelope, with the earth at its center and the celestial bodies, including the stars, the sun and the planets, revolving around it. This geocentric view of the universe was elaborated with great ingenuity by Ptolemy and his followers into a complex astronomical theory that was able to predict the movements of the heavenly bodies with remarkable accuracy.

Nevertheless, by the time Copernicus turned his attention to the study of the heavens, astronomers had compiled a large mass of detailed observations, principally concerning the locations of the planets and the precession of the equinoxes, that the Ptolemaic view could not comfortably account for.

In 1543, Copernicus published his *De Revolutionibus* which proposed that the known astronomical observations could be explained better by supposing that the earth rotated on its own axis once a day and revolved around the sun once a year. Several decades later, Galileo, using one of the first astronomical telescopes, produced dramatic evidence in favor of Copernicus' theory. The Copernican view suggested that the planets should resemble earth, that earth is not the only center around which heavenly bodies revolve, that Venus would exhibit phases and that the universe is vastly larger than had previously been supposed. When Galileo's telescope revealed mountains on the moon, the moons of Jupiter, the phases of Venus and a huge number of previously unsuspected stars, the stage seemed set for a radical reconception of the universe.

For his efforts, Galileo was summoned to Rome in 1615, to defend his views against the charge of heresy.[1] The Vatican's case was prosecuted by the infamous Cardinal Bellarmine, who when invited by Galileo to look through his telescope to see for himself, is reputed to have refused, saying that he had a far better source of evidence about the make-up of the heavens, namely, the Holy Scripture itself.

Commenting on this incident, Rorty writes:

But can we then find a way of saying that the considerations advanced against the Copernican theory by Cardinal Bellarmine—the scriptural description of the fabric of the heavens—were "illogical or unscientific?" ...[Bellarmine] defended his view by saying that we had excellent independent (scriptural) evidence for believing that the heavens were roughly Ptolemaic. Was his evidence brought in from another

---

[1] For a gripping account of this episode in the history of thought, see Giorgio de Santillana, *The Crime of Galileo* (Chicago: University of Chicago Press, 1955).

sphere, and was his proposed restriction of scope thus "unscientific?" What determines that Scripture is not an excellent source of evidence for the way the heavens are set up?[2]

Rorty answers his own questions as follows:

So the question about whether Bellarmine ... was bringing in extraneous "unscientific" considerations seems to me to be a question about whether there is some antecedent way of determining the relevance of one statement to another, some "grid" (to use Foucault's term) which determines what sorts of evidence there could be for statements about the movements of planets.

Obviously, the conclusion I wish to draw is that the "grid" which emerged in the later seventeenth and eighteenth centuries was not there to be appealed to in the early seventeenth century, at the time that Galileo was on trial. No conceivable epistemology, no study of the nature of human knowledge, could have "discovered" it before it was hammered out. The notion of what it was to be "scientific" was in the process of being formed. If one endorses the values ... common to Galileo and Kant, then indeed Bellarmine was being "unscientific." But, of course, almost all of us ... are happy to endorse them. We are the heirs of three hundred years of rhetoric about the importance of distinguishing sharply between science and religion, science and politics, science and philosophy, and so on. This rhetoric has formed the culture of Europe. It made us what we are today. We are fortunate that no little perplexity within epistemology, or within the historiography of science, is enough to defeat it. But to proclaim our loyalty to these distinctions is not to say that there are "objective" and "rational" standards for adopting them. Galileo, so to speak, won the argument, and we all stand on the common ground of the "grid" of relevance and irrelevance which "modern philosophy" developed as a consequence of that victory. But what could show that the Bellarmine-Galileo issue "differs in kind" from the issue between, say, Kerensky and Lenin, or that between the Royal Academy (circa 1910) and Bloomsbury?[3]

[2] Richard Rorty, *Philosophy and the Mirror of Nature* (Princeton: Princeton University Press, 1981), 328–9.
[3] ibid. 330–1.

In these arresting passages, Rorty expresses the central tenets of a constructivist/relativist view of justified belief.[4] Galileo asserts that he has evidence which justifies belief in Copernicanism. Bellarmine denies this, claiming that he has a better source of evidence about the make-up of the heavens than Galileo's observations, namely, the Holy Scripture itself. According to Rorty, there is no fact of the matter about which of these antagonists is right, for there are no absolute facts about what justifies what. Rather, Bellarmine and Galileo are operating with fundamentally different *epistemic systems*—fundamentally different "grids" for determining "what sorts of evidence there could be for statements about the movements of planets." And there is no fact of the matter as to which of their systems is "correct"—a fact that some epistemology might discover—just as there is no fact that can help settle the political dispute between the Mensheviks and the Bolsheviks or the aesthetic dispute between members of the Bloomsbury Group and the Royal Academy.

Rorty acknowledges that, having come to adopt Galileo's system, we now reject Bellarmine's and call it "unscientific" and "illogical." According to Rorty, however, this is just a sophisticated form of name-calling: all we're doing is expressing our preference for Galileo's system and rejecting Bellarmine's: there can be no "objective ... standards" by virtue of which Galileo's system is better than Bellarmine's, more accurately reflective of the objective facts about justification. If our judgments about what it's "rational" to believe are to have any prospect of being true, we should not claim that some belief (e.g. Copernicanism) is justified absolutely by the available

[4] There are other positions in the literature that have claimed this label. In this book, I shall concentrate on the sort of epistemic relativism that Rorty describes in this passage—a relativism that insists on relativizing epistemic judgments to the background epistemic conceptions employed by diverse thinkers, to their respective "grids" of epistemic relevance and irrelevance, in Rorty's language. I will have something to say about alternative formulations in the next chapter.

evidence (e.g. Galileo's observations), but only that it is justified relative to the particular epistemic system that we have come to accept.

Notice that this relativistic view is untouched by the arguments of the previous chapters because it proposes only to relativize facts about justified beliefs and not all facts as such.

And notice, also, how concessive such a view can afford to be to the objectivism about facts that we were insisting on in the previous chapter. Sure, there may be a fact of the matter about whether the heavens are Copernican or Ptolemaic. But there is no absolute fact of the matter, such a relativist may argue, about which of those views it would be most rational for someone to have. The only absolute truths in the vicinity are truths about what is permitted by this or that epistemic system, with different people finding different epistemic systems attractive.

If such a constructivist/relativistic view of justification could be sustained, it would look to give immediate support to the idea that there are many radically different, yet equally valid ways of knowing the world.[5] Moreover, and as I have already mentioned, there appears to be a seductively powerful argument in its support. I propose, therefore, to devote considerable attention to it in the next three chapters.

Epistemic Systems and Practices

Galileo, Rorty says, "won the argument, and we all stand on the common ground of the 'grid' of relevance and irrelevance which 'modern philosophy' developed as a consequence of that

[5] The relativist should avoid the trap of saying that this is because such a view would show that there are many radically different, yet equally *rational*, ways of knowing the world, for that would amount to endorsing a use of "rational" that is absolute—whereas the relativist view on offer is precisely that we cannot sensibly speak of what is rational, period, but only of what is rational relative to this or that accepted epistemic system.

victory." Let us begin by taking a closer look at the "grid" on which we, post-Galileans, are supposed to stand.

Just about any reader of this book, I conjecture, will recognize the following to be a principle that he or she relies upon in forming beliefs, or in assessing the beliefs of others:

(Observation-dog) If it visually appears to a thinker S that there is a dog in front of him, then S is prima facie justified in believing that there is a dog in front of him.

Several points are in order, even with respect to such a simple example. First, the actual principle we endorse is nothing as straightforward as Observation-dog. Various other conditions—some pertaining to the state of the thinker's visual apparatus, others pertaining to the environmental circumstances—would also have to be satisfied. If, for example, we have reason to distrust the operation of our senses on a given occasion, or if the lighting conditions are poor, we would not think it justified to believe that there is a dog in front of us, even if it so seemed. So when I say that we endorse a principle that permits belief on the basis of observation, I mean something that is subject to a number of complicated provisos, something more like:

(Observation-dog 2) If it visually seems to S that there is a dog in front of him, and circumstantial conditions D obtain, then S is prima facie justified in believing that there is a dog in front of him.

Second, there is, of course, nothing special about beliefs involving dogs. Rather, we take there to be a certain range of propositional contents—*observational* contents—belief in which is reasonably secured on the basis of observation:

(Observation) For any observational proposition p, if it visually seems to S that p and circumstantial conditions D obtain, then S is prima facie justified in believing p.

It is not easy to be precise about which propositional contents are observational in this sense, but our commitment to the existence of some such distinction is clear enough (propositions about the shapes of middle-sized objects count, whereas those about sub-atomic particles don't).

Finally, and as we have just seen, it is hard to say, even as a purely descriptive matter, precisely which epistemic principles we operate with. In their full detail, these principles are enormously complicated and even philosophers who have worked on the topic for years would be hard pressed to formulate them in a way that is free of counterexamples. In what sense, then, could we say that these rules constitute *our* epistemic practice?

Clearly, the idea is not that we *grasp* Observation explicitly, as we would some ordinary proposition; rather, the idea is that we *operate according to* Observation: it is *implicit* in our practice, rather than explicit in our formulations. We operate according to this principle even if we are unable to say, if asked, exactly which principle it is that we are following. The phenomenon is by no means confined to the case of knowledge. Our *linguistic* behavior is equally under the control of an enormously complex system of principles of which we lack as yet a fully adequate representation.[6]

Observation is an example of a "generation" principle—it generates a justified belief on the basis of something that is not itself a belief but rather a perceptual state. Many of the epistemic principles we operate with are "transmission" principles, principles that prescribe how to move from some justified beliefs to other justified beliefs.

---

[6] I have been talking about our following norms or principles. It is more common to talk about our following *rules*, which are expressed by imperatives of the form "If C, do A", rather than principles, which are typically expressed by indicative sentences. I cannot here explain why I have avoided rule-talk, except to say that there are many things that we call rules—such as the rule for castling in chess—which are expressed by indicatives rather than imperatives.

One example of such a transmission principle has to do with moving across what we take to be *deductively valid* inferences, inferences which are such that, if their premises are true, their conclusions must be true as well. For example:

(Modus Ponens-rain) If S justifiably believes that it will rain tomorrow, and justifiably believes that if it rains tomorrow the streets will be wet tomorrow, S is justified in believing that the streets will be wet tomorrow.

Another example is given by the principle of conjunction-elimination:

(Conjunction-elimination-rain) If S justifiably believes that it will be cold and rainy tomorrow, then S is justified in believing that it will be cold tomorrow.

More generally, we endorse the principle that thinkers are justified in believing the obvious logical consequences of beliefs they are justified in having.

(Deduction) If S is justified in believing p and p fairly obviously entails q, then S is justified in believing q.

(As before, a large number of delicate qualifications would have to be entered for this to capture the exact principle we operate with, but they will not matter for our purposes.)[7]

Although much of our reasoning is deductive, much of it isn't and couldn't be. If we ask how we know that whenever it rains the streets get wet, the answer is *experience*: it's a regularity that we've observed. But as David Hume pointed out, our experience only speaks to what has been true about the past and to what has been true in our immediate vicinity. When we use our experience with rain to predict how things will be tomorrow when it rains, or when we use it to form beliefs about how things are in

[7] For some discussion of the qualifications that might be needed see Gilbert Harman, "Rationality," in his *Reasoning, Meaning, and Mind* (Oxford: Clarendon Press, 1999), 9–45, and Gilbert Harman, *Changes in View: Principles of Reasoning* (Cambridge, Mass.: The MIT Press, 1986), ch. 1.

places far away from us, we are not reasoning deductively but rather *inductively*. The claim

Whenever it has rained in the past the streets have become wet

does not logically entail

Whenever it rains in the future, the streets will get wet.

It is not, strictly speaking, a logical contradiction to maintain that, although wet streets have always succeeded rain in the past they will fail to do so in the future. That prospect may seem bizarre, but it is not self-contradictory. Rather, our assumption is that our experience with rain here and now gives us a good but non-conclusive reason for forming beliefs about rain there and then. We may express our practice here through the principle of

(Induction) If S has often enough observed that an event of type A has been followed by an event of type B, then S is justified in believing that all events of type A will be followed by events of type B.

Needless to say by now, Induction, as stated, is very rough and stands in need of various qualifications that need not detain us.

Between them, Observation, Deduction and Induction specify a significant portion, even if not the whole, of the *fundamental* principles of our ordinary, "post-Galilean" epistemic system. (The way of fixing beliefs that we call "science" is in large part a rigorous application of these ordinary, familiar principles.) By a "fundamental" principle, I mean a principle whose correctness cannot be derived from the correctness of other epistemic principles. Since the distinction between fundamental and derived epistemic principles is important to what follows, let me dwell on it for a moment.

Suppose that by using some of the ordinary epistemic principles I have been describing, I conclude that Nora is a very reliable guide to what live music might be available on any given evening in New York. Every time I have asked her, she has turned out to have all the information at her fingertips and it has always been accurate as verified by observation and so forth. On that basis, I would be justified in operating according to a new epistemic principle:

> (Nora) Regarding propositions about what live music is available on any given evening in NY, if Nora says that p to S then S is justified in believing p.

Clearly, though, my endorsement of this principle would not be fundamental to my epistemic system but would rather derive from my acceptance of these other principles: were it not for them, I would not have come to accept Nora.

Observation, by contrast, seems not to be like that: its status seems rather to be basic and underived. Any evidence in support of Observation, it would seem, would have to rely on Observation itself.

In what follows, we shall naturally be especially interested in the fundamental principles, in those that can be justified, if at all, only by appeal to themselves.

Some philosophers would insist on recognizing yet further fundamental principles in our ordinary epistemic system:

> (Inference to the best explanation) If S justifiably believes that p, and justifiably believes that the *best explanation* for p is q, then S is justified in believing q.

Others will want to incorporate various assumptions about the role of *simplicity* in our thinking. Others still will want to complicate the picture further by talking not so much about belief but about *degrees of belief*, and about the role that assumptions about probability play in fixing them.

We could go much further in attempting to fill in this picture of our ordinary epistemic system; but we don't need to for present purposes. We already have enough with which to engage the relativist's claim that there are no absolute facts about what justifies what, but only relational facts about what is allowed or forbidden by particular epistemic systems.

Let us return briefly to the dispute between Galileo and Cardinal Bellarmine. It is not immediately clear from Rorty's description how we should characterize the alternative epistemic system to which Bellarmine is said to adhere. A plausible suggestion would be that among its fundamental principles is the following:

(Revelation) For certain propositions p, including propositions about the heavens, believing p is prima facie justified if p is the revealed word of God as claimed by the Bible.

And so, since the Bible apparently says that the heavens are Ptolemaic, that is what we are justified in believing. In contrast, I take it, *we* would think that even the ostensibly revealed word of God should give way to the theories that were arrived at through such principles as Observation, Induction, Deduction and inference to the best explanation.

Very few ordinary (non-fundamentalist) members of contemporary Western society would advocate substituting the Scriptural view of the heavens for the picture disclosed by science. Nor would we regard with equanimity anyone who would.

Rorty acknowledges that we do not take a tolerant view of the disagreement to which these two conceptions give rise. He echoes Wittgenstein who says in his *On Certainty*:

611. Where two principles really do meet which cannot be reconciled with one another, then each man declares the other a fool and a heretic.[8]

He insists, however, that all this rhetorical heat simply covers up the fact that there is no system-independent fact in virtue of which one epistemic system could be said to be more correct than any other.

[8] Ludwig Wittgenstein, *On Certainty*, ed. G. E. M. Anscombe and G. H. von Wright, trans. Denis Paul and G. E. M. Anscombe (Oxford: Basil Blackwell, 1975).

Wittgenstein and the Azande

The wider context for the passage from Wittgenstein just quoted is the following series of remarks from *On Certainty*:

608. Is it wrong for me to be guided in my actions by the propositions of physics? Am I to say I have no good ground for doing so? Isn't precisely this what we call a 'good ground'?

609. Supposing we met people who did not regard that as a telling reason. Now, how do we imagine this? Instead of the physicist, they consult an oracle. (And for that we consider them primitive.) Is it wrong for them to consult an oracle and be guided by it?—If we call this 'wrong' aren't we using our language-game as a base from which to *combat* theirs?

610. And are we right or wrong to combat it? Of course there are all sorts of slogans which will be used to support our proceedings.

611. Where two principles really do meet which cannot be reconciled with one another, then each man declares the other a fool and a heretic.

612. I said I would 'combat' the other man,—but wouldn't I offer him *reasons?* Certainly, but how far would they go? At the end of reasons comes *persuasion.* (Think what happens when missionaries convert natives.)

Although Wittgenstein presents his community of oracle consulters as though it were merely imaginary, he was intimately familiar, through the writings of anthropologists like James G. Frazer and E. E. Evans-Pritchard, with real-life examples.[9]

Look at the case of the Azande studied by Evans-Pritchard. According to his account, there are many respects in which the Azande are just like ordinary Westerners, sharing many of our ordinary beliefs about the world. For example, they believe that the shadow cast by a granary can provide relief from summer heat, that termites are capable of eating away at the legs of

[9] See James G. Frazer, *The Golden Bough: A Study in Magic and Religion*, 3rd edn. reprint of the 1911 edn. (New York: Macmillan, 1980) and E. E. Evans-Pritchard, *Witchcraft, Oracles and Magic among the Azande* (Oxford: Clarendon Press, 1937).

granaries so that they sometimes fall down unexpectedly, and that large, heavy objects falling on someone can injure them.

However, when a granary falls on someone who is sheltering under it, the Azande don't talk about these natural causes but attribute the misfortune rather to witchcraft. On their view, all calamities are to be explained by invoking witchcraft.

A witch, the Azande further believe, is a (typically male) member of their own community who has a special witchcraft substance in his belly. This substance, they maintain, is transmitted by a male witch to all his male descendants and can be detected visually in post-mortem examinations. If a witch attack is particularly serious, an effort is made to determine who might have been responsible.

To answer this question, a close kinsman of the victim takes the name of a possible suspect to an oracle and a 'yes/no' question is put to him. Simultaneously, a small amount of poison is administered to a chicken. Depending on how the chicken dies, the oracle is able to say whether the answer to the question is positive or negative. This procedure is followed not only with respect to questions about witchcraft, but with respect to most questions that are of significance to the Azande.

It looks, then, as though with respect to a significant range of propositions—who caused this calamity? will it rain tomorrow? will the hunt be successful?—the Azande employ a significantly different epistemic principle than we would. Instead of reasoning via explanation, induction and so forth, they seem to employ the principle:

(Oracle) For certain propositions p, believing p is prima facie justified if a Poison Oracle says that p.

This practice certainly seems to contrast with our own epistemic procedures; whether it amounts to a fundamental alternative to our epistemic system is a question to which I shall return; for now, I will simply go along with the assumption that it is.

Some scholars have maintained that the Azande differ from us in another important respect as well—they have a different deductive *logic* from ours.

Recall the Azande belief that witchcraft substance is inherited patrilineally. It would seem to follow from this that one clear-cut case of witchcraft identification is all it would take to establish that an entire lineage of people have been or will be witches. The reasoning would proceed by modus ponens. If x is a witch, then all of x's patrilineal male descendants are witches. x is a witch (independently confirmed, let's suppose, by the oracle or by a post-mortem). Therefore, all of these male descendants must be witches as well.

The Azande, however, do not seem to accept these inferences. As Evans-Pritchard put it:

> To our minds it appears evident that if a man is proven a witch the whole of his clan are ipso facto witches, since the Zande clan is a group of persons related biologically through the male line. Azande see the sense of this argument but they do not accept its conclusions, and it would involve the whole notion of witchcraft in contradiction were they to do so.[10]

Apparently, the Azande accept only that the close paternal kinsmen of a known witch are also witches. Some scholars have concluded from this that the Azande employ a different logic from ours, one that involves rejecting unqualified use of modus ponens.[11]

Defending Epistemic Relativism

Let us accept for now the claim that Azande and the Vatican circa 1630 represent the use of *fundamentally* different epistemic systems: their underived epistemic principles diverge from ours.

[10] Evans-Pritchard, *Witchcraft, Oracles and Magic among the Azande*, 34.
[11] David Bloor, *Knowledge and Social Imagery*, 2nd edn. (Chicago, University of Chicago Press, 1991), 138–40.

Let us also accept that these systems are what I shall call *genuine* alternatives to ours: on a given range of propositions and fixed evidential circumstances, they yield *conflicting* verdicts on what it is justified to believe. (It's important to add this condition at this point, for we want to make sure that the epistemic systems that concern us not only differ from each other but that they rule on the justifiability of a given belief in mutually incompatible ways.)

Using the template we developed in the previous chapter, we can formulate epistemic relativism as follows:

Epistemic Relativism:

A. There are no absolute facts about what belief a particular item of information justifies. (Epistemic non-absolutism)

B. If a person, S's, epistemic judgments are to have any prospect of being true, we must not construe his utterances of the form

> "E justifies belief B"

as expressing the claim

> *E justifies belief B*

but rather as expressing the claim:

> *According to the epistemic system C, that I, S, accept, information E justifies belief B.* (Epistemic relationism)

C. There are many fundamentally different, genuinely alternative epistemic systems, but no facts by virtue of which one of these systems is more correct than any of the others. (Epistemic pluralism)

Now, there are many prima facie puzzling aspects to epistemic relativism as so formulated—but I propose not to dwell on them now but to come back to them after we have had a chance to appreciate the positive case that can be made in its favor. In marked contrast with a relativism about facts in general, which as we saw is very difficult to defend, I believe that a very strong prima facie case can be made for epistemic relativism. It is given by the following argument:

Argument for Epistemic Relativism

1. If there are absolute epistemic facts about what justifies what, then it ought to be possible to arrive at justified beliefs about them.

2. It is not possible to arrive at justified beliefs about what absolute epistemic facts there are.

   Therefore,

3. There are no absolute epistemic facts. (Epistemic non-absolutism)

4. If there are no absolute epistemic facts, then epistemic relativism is true.

   Therefore,

5. Epistemic relativism is true.

This argument is evidently valid; the only question is whether it is sound.

I propose immediately to sidestep premise 4. Since the issues it raises are subtle and potentially distracting, I am simply going to grant it for the purposes of this discussion. Let me explain.

According to epistemic relativism, as I have construed it, when we say something of the form

($) "E justifies belief B"

we intend to be making a factual judgment capable of being assessed as true or false. Since according to non-absolutism, there is no unrelativized fact of that form for the sentence to report, the relativist urges us to reconstrue such judgments as making only relational judgments about what various epistemic systems require or permit.

However, as we had occasion to note in the previous chapter, there have been philosophers who have thought that normative statements in general—and so epistemic statements in particular—are not in the business of making factual judgments. According to these philosophers, judgments of the form ($) are rather to be understood as expressing the thinker's states of mind—according to Allan Gibbard's well-known proposal, for example, as expressing the thinker's acceptance of a system of norms that permits believing B under conditions E.[12] We may call such philosophers *expressivists* about epistemic judgments. An expressivist in this sense may well want to accept epistemic non-absolutism; but he would resist the second clause of the relativist's view which recommends reconstruing epistemic judgments as relational judgments.

Now, the question whether there really is such an expressivist option in the epistemic case or elsewhere and the question whether it amounts to a compelling view of normative judgments, are large questions that I cannot hope to enter into here.[13] For the purpose of giving the epistemic relativist the strongest possible hand, I propose simply to grant premise 4 for the purposes of this discussion. Thus, I will take it that epistemic relativism will have been secured once we have made a plausible case for epistemic non-absolutism. The question I shall consider is whether such a case is forthcoming.

Let us turn our attention then to the two premises on which the case for non-absolutism depends, beginning with the first. According to this premise, if there are absolute epistemic facts, it must be possible to come to have justified beliefs about what those facts are.

It is possible to hear this as making a stronger claim than is actually intended.

It is not crucial to the first premise that we be able to know which absolute epistemic facts obtain in their full detail. Perhaps the norms that specify when a belief is justified are so extraordinarily complicated that it would take an enormous idealization

12 Allan Gibbard, *Wise Choices, Apt Feelings: A Theory of Normative Judgement* (Cambridge, Mass.: Harvard University Press, 1990).
13 For some discussion, see my "How are Objective Epistemic Reasons Possible?" *Philosophical Studies* 106 (2001): 1–40.

of our actual powers to figure out what they are in full detail. It is enough for the purposes of this premise that we be able to know them in rough approximation, that we be able to rule out *radical* alternatives, even if we are unable to decide between two very close contenders.

When the first premise is qualified in this way, it seems hardly to need any defense. Whenever we confidently judge that some belief is justified on the basis of a given piece of information, we are tacitly assuming that such facts are not only knowable but that they are known. And in doing epistemology, we not only assume that they are knowable, we assume that they are knowable a priori. Indeed, what would be the interest of an absolutism about epistemic truths which combined that absolutism with the affirmation that those truths are necessarily inaccessible to us? (Compare: what would be the interest of an absolutism about moral truths which combined it with the affirmation that those absolute truths are necessarily inaccessible to us?)

Suppose, then, that we grant the first premise, either because it seems plausible, or because we so define epistemic absolutism that it already includes the (rough) epistemic accessibility of facts about justification. Still, why should we grant the argument's second premise, that such facts are not knowable?

Consider a situation in which a disagreement arises about what the absolute epistemic facts are. We encounter Bellarmine, or the Azande, and they question whether our view of those facts is correct. They say we are mistaken to think that Galileo's observations justify Copernicanism. We, for our part, think they are mistaken to deny it. If there really were a fact of the matter here, we have said, we ought to be able to settle it one way or the other. How, though, could we show them the error of their views?

Our first move, of course, would be to show that our judgment that

Such-and-so considerations justify Copernicanism

follows from the general epistemic principles that we accept, from our epistemic system. But that just pushes the crucial question back. Why think that our epistemic system is correct and theirs isn't? How do we now tackle that question?

To show them—or ourselves, for that matter—that our system is correct and theirs wrong, we would have to *justify* the principles of our system over theirs, we would have to offer them some *argument* that demonstrated the objective superiority of our system over theirs. But any such argument would require using an epistemic system, relying on the cogency of some epistemic principles and not others. Which system should we use?

Well, naturally, we would use ours. We take ours to be the correct system; we think theirs is mistaken. That's exactly what we are trying to show. We could hardly hope to show that we are justified in thinking our system correct by justifying it with the use of a system that doesn't yield justified verdicts.

But also naturally, *they* would use *their* system to decide which of us is right.

Suppose now that we each discover that our own principles decide in favor of themselves and against the other practice. This is not exactly a foregone conclusion since some sets of principles will be *self-undermining*, ruling against themselves, and others may be *tolerant* of some degree of divergence. But it is a very likely outcome for any sufficiently well-developed epistemic system.

On that scenario, then, we will have two self-supporting practices that are at odds with each other. Will we have shown anything substantive; could we really claim to have demonstrated that our principles are correct, and theirs not? Is either one of us in a position to call the other 'wrong'?

Think of what Wittgenstein says:

Is it wrong for them to consult an oracle and be guided by it?—If we call this 'wrong' aren't we using our language-game as a base from which to *combat* theirs?

If we persist in calling them wrong, Wittgenstein is saying, we are simply *insisting* on the superiority of our practice over theirs; we could not honestly claim to have rationally demonstrated that their system is mistaken.

Now, there are two different ways of hearing this charge of Wittgenstein's, one of which is less threatening to epistemic absolutism than the other.

On the less threatening interpretation, we could understand him to say: well, although you may have shown something about the superiority of your system over your opponents', your demonstration is dialectically ineffective: your opponents will remain thoroughly unpersuaded and they would have every right to do so since your demonstration begs the question against them. You may have shown something substantive by *your* lights, but not by *theirs*.

To this objection, the objectivist could reasonably reply: perhaps you are right, but if so that is their problem. It's not my fault that they are so far gone that my perfectly reasonable arguments are unable to reach them.

But there is another more potent reading of Wittgenstein's charge according to which our argument would not have shown anything about the correctness of our own system, even *by our own lights*, and not just by the lights of our opponents.

The point is that *we ourselves* seem to acknowledge that we cannot hope to demonstrate the correctness of an epistemic system by using *that very system*. As Richard Fumerton has put it,

...there is no philosophically interesting notion of justification or knowledge that would allow us to use a kind of reasoning to justify the legitimacy of using that reasoning.[14]

Fumerton is surely onto something. If we really do take our confrontation with an alien epistemic system to throw our system into doubt, and so to call for a genuine justification of that system, how could we possibly hope to advance that project by showing that our system is ruled correct by itself? If we have reason to doubt whether our principles yield genuinely justified beliefs, why should we be comforted by the fact that we can construct an argument in their favor that relies on them? To doubt them is precisely to doubt the value of the beliefs that are arrived at on their basis.

If these considerations are right, then it looks as though, *even by our own lights*, we cannot hope to settle the question which epistemic system is correct, once it has been raised. We consequently seem to have to concede that, if there are objective facts about justification, those facts are in principle unknowable.[15]

And with that the relativist's argument goes through. The most that any epistemic practice will be able to say, when confronted by a fundamentally different, genuine alternative, self-supporting epistemic practice, is that it is correct by its own lights, whereas the alternative isn't. But that cannot yield a *justification* of the one practice over the other, without begging the question. If the point is to decide which of the two practices is better than the other, self-certification is not going to help. Each side will be able to provide a *norm-circular* justification of its own practice; neither side will be able to provide anything more. With what right, then, could either party claim to have a superior

<hr/>

[14] Richard Fumerton, *Metaepistemology and Skepticism* (Lanham, Md.: Rowman & Littlefield, 1995), 180.

[15] In presenting this pro-relativist argument, I am deliberately eliding certain important distinctions—we will return to those distinctions in chapter 7.

conception of rational or justified belief? We seem left with no choice but to say, as Wittgenstein does in his *Philosophical Investigations:*

> If I have exhausted the justifications I have reached bedrock, and my spade is turned. Then I am inclined to say: "This is simply what I do."[16]

[16] Ludwig Wittgenstein, *Philosophical Investigations*, trans. G. E. M. Anscombe (Oxford: Blackwell, 1953), para. 217.

6

Epistemic Relativism Rejected

Reason versus Reasons

In his book on the objectivity of reason, Thomas Nagel professes not to be disturbed by such arguments from norm-circularity:

if someone responds to every challenge to tea-leaf reading as a method of deciding factual or practical questions by appealing to further consultation of the tea leaves, it would be thought absurd. Why is reasoning about challenges to reason different?[1]

Nagel answers his own question as follows:

The answer is that the appeal to reason is implicitly authorized by the challenge itself, so this is really a way of showing that the challenge is unintelligible. The charge of begging the question implies that there is an alternative—namely, to examine the reasons for and against the claim being challenged while suspending judgment about it. For the case of reasoning itself, however, no such alternative is available, since any considerations against the objective validity of a type of reasoning

---

[1] Nagel, *The Last Word*, 24.

are inevitably attempts to offer reasons against it, and these must be rationally assessed. The use of reason in the response is not a gratuitous importation by the defender: It is demanded by the character of the objections offered by the challenger. In contrast, a challenge to the authority of tea leaves does not itself lead us back to the tea leaves.[2]

Nagel's observations constitute an effective rejoinder to someone who would challenge the very point of looking for and offering reasons for our beliefs. Against such a skeptic, he correctly points out, the use of reason is authorized by the challenge itself, for the skeptic has no choice but to present himself as having reasons for doubting their effectiveness.

The problem of norm-circularity, however, is not in the first instance a challenge to reason itself, but a challenge to the objective validity of specific forms of reasoning. The tea-leaf reader need not be presented as an irrationalist, repudiating reason as such, but rather as offering an alternative form of reasoning. If we maintain that this alternative form of reasoning does not in fact provide genuine justifications for its conclusions, we must explain in what the superiority of our own methods consists. If, however, the most we can say in their support is something norm-circular, wouldn't that be equally available to the tea-leaf reader?[3]

The problem posed by norm-circularity for the epistemic objectivist is not so easily dispatched. Nevertheless, I agree with Nagel that epistemic relativism is not a tenable view. What is wrong with it?

A Traditional Refutation

We have already had occasion to look at traditional refutations of a relativism about truth in the previous chapter. Translated into terms that are more directly relevant to our current concern with

[2] Nagel, *The Last Word*, 24.

[3] Once again, the claim is not that all epistemic norms can be counted on to be self-supporting, just that quite a few radically alternative ones will be.

epistemic justification, that traditional refutation would look something like this:

The claim "Nothing is objectively justified, but only justified relative to this or that epistemic system" must be nonsense, for it would itself have to be either objectively justified, or only justified relative to this or that particular epistemic system. But it can't be objectively justified, since in that case it would be false if true. And it can't be justified only relative to the relativist's epistemic system, since in that case it is just a report of what he finds it agreeable to say. If he also invites us to join him, we need not offer any reason for declining since he has offered us no reason to accept.

Once again, though, the flaw is in the argument against the subjectivist horn. If the relativist opts for saying that relativism is justified only relative to his (the relativist's) epistemic principles, it doesn't immediately follow that he is just saying what "he finds it agreeable to say." Indeed, it doesn't even follow that he is saying that relativism is justified only relative to epistemic principles that are *unique* to relativists. For all we are entitled to assume, he may mean that relativism is justified by a set of principles that are endorsed by relativists and non-relativists alike. So we are not immediately entitled to say that, if the relativist opts for this horn, we are entitled to ignore him.

Indeed, as we have already seen, the pro-relativist argument of the previous chapter relies only on two assumptions.

First, that in evaluating an epistemic system there is no alternative but to use some epistemic system or other. And second, that there is no interesting notion of justification that will allow us to justify a form of reasoning through the use of that very form of reasoning. Both assumptions seem plausible; they certainly seem plausible to *us*. If the relativist defends his view by appealing to that argument, we can hardly dismiss him by saying that his view is justified only for relativists; his view would appear to have been justified for all of us.

With what right, then, does the objectivist claim the freedom simply to ignore the relativism that those principles appear to support?

Accepting an Epistemic System

Even if these traditional objections to epistemic relativism don't work especially well, others do.

Let us begin by looking at particular unrelativized epistemic judgments, such as:

1. Copernicanism is justified by Galileo's observations.

The relativist says that all such judgments are doomed to falsehood because there are no absolute facts about justification. If we are to retain epistemic discourse, the relativist urges, we must reform our talk so that we no longer speak simply about what is justified by the evidence, but only about what is justified by the evidence according to the particular epistemic system that we happen to accept, noting, all the while, that there are no facts by virtue of which our particular system is more correct than any of the others. Hence:

Epistemic Relativism
   A. There are no absolute facts about what belief a particular item of information justifies. (Epistemic non-absolutism)
   B. If a person, S's, epistemic judgments are to have any prospect of being true, we must not construe his utterances of the form
      "E justifies belief B"
as expressing the claim
      E justifies belief B
      but rather as expressing the claim:
   According to the epistemic system C, that I, S, accept, information E justifies belief B. (Epistemic relationism)

C. There are many fundamentally different, genuinely alternative epistemic systems, but no facts by virtue of which one of these systems is more correct than any of the others. (Epistemic pluralism)

Thus, if we accept the relativist's recommendation, we would no longer assert (1) but only:

2. Copernicanism is justified by Galileo's observations relative to a system, Science, that, I, the speaker, accept.

Now, an epistemic system, we have said, consists of a set of general normative propositions—epistemic principles—which specify under which conditions a particular type of belief is justified. Whereas a *particular* epistemic judgment might speak of particular people, beliefs and evidential conditions, as in:

3. If it visually seems to Galileo that there are mountains on the moon, then Galileo is justified in believing that there are mountains on the moon;

an epistemic principle will say something general like:

(Observation) For any observational proposition p, if it visually seems to S that p and circumstantial conditions D obtain, then S is prima facie justified in believing p.

In other words, and as we can plainly see, the epistemic principles which constitute particular epistemic systems are just more *general* versions of particular epistemic judgments. They, too, are propositions stating the conditions under which a belief would be absolutely justified, the only difference being that they do so in a very general way and without adverting to particular beliefs held by particular agents at particular times and under particular evidential conditions.

Now, however, if the relativist's central thought is that particular epistemic judgments are *uniformly false,* and so must be replaced by judgments about what is entailed by the epistemic systems that we happen to accept, then it follows from this central thought that the general epistemic principles which constitute the epistemic systems that we accept must be false, too, for they are general propositions of much the same type.

If the relation between a particular epistemic judgment and an epistemic principle is like the relation between the proposition

4. Jack is immortal

and the proposition

5. All men are immortal

then, if someone says that every instance of (4) is false, there is no choice but to think that (5) is false, too. There is simply no room for maneuver here.

Well, suppose that we take that point on board, and so agree that the various general epistemic principles out of which epistemic systems are composed are themselves false. Why should that cause any problems for the relativist? Even if epistemic systems are made up out of false propositions, there can still be true statements about what those false propositions do and do not entail.

The trouble is that, as we have already seen, it is crucial to the relativist's view that thinkers *accept* one or another of these systems, that they *endorse* one or another of them and then talk about what they do and do not permit. Otherwise we could not even make sense of the idea that Galileo thinks he has a *relative* reason for believing Copernicanism while Bellarmine thinks he has a relative reason for rejecting it.

But how could we go on accepting one or another of these epistemic systems, once we have bought in on the relativist's central thought that there are no absolute facts about justification and so have come to conclude that they are made up out of uniformly false propositions?

The relativist says that we should stop making absolute judgments about what justifies what and that we should stick to saying what epistemic judgments follow from the epistemic systems we accept.

But it is hard to see how we might coherently follow this advice. Given that the propositions which make up epistemic systems are just very general propositions about what absolutely justifies what, it makes no sense to insist that we abandon making absolute *particular* judgments about what justifies what while allowing us to *accept* absolute *general* judgments about what justifies what. But that is, in effect, what the epistemic relativist is recommending.

It is also hard to explain why anyone should care about what follows from a set of propositions that are acknowledged to be uniformly false. What sort of normative authority over us could an epistemic system exert, once we have become convinced that it is made up of propositions that are uniformly false?

Epistemic relativism looks to be an incoherent response to the putative discovery that there are no absolute facts about epistemic justification.

Epistemic Systems as Sets of Incomplete Propositions?

All of these problems for epistemic relativism trace back to the assumption that ordinary epistemic utterances, such as,

1. Copernicanism is justified by Galileo's observations

express complete truth-evaluable propositions. Once that assumption is in place, there is no alternative for the relativist but to say that such judgments are uniformly false and no alternative but to take a relativistic conception of them as involving their entailment by a set of similar, though more general, false propositions.

The question, therefore, quickly suggests itself: is that assumption optional?

It might look as though it is. Here is the thought: To get away from absolute facts about epistemic justification, all we really need is for judgments of the form

Copernicanism is justified by Galileo's observations

to be *untrue*; it is not strictly speaking required that we think of those judgments as *false*. But there are two ways, of course, for a judgment to be untrue, only one of which consists in its being false. The other way is for the judgment to be untrue because *incomplete*. Consider, for example, the proposition-fragment:

Tom is taller than . . .

This proposition cannot be true, not because it is false but because it is an incomplete proposition-fragment that cannot be evaluated for truth. It is untrue because incomplete.

This suggests an alternative way of formulating epistemic relativism. Suppose we say that the relativist's central thought is that statements like (1) are untrue because incomplete. What the relativist has discovered is that they need to be completed by reference to an epistemic system before they can sensibly be appraised for truth. Wouldn't this alternative evade the difficulties we have recently been exposing?

Well, suppose we say that a proposition of the form

Copernicanism is justified by Galileo's observations

is an incomplete proposition, in much the way that

Tom is taller than . . .

is clearly incomplete. And suppose we try to complete it with:

In relation to epistemic system C, Copernicanism is justified by Galileo's observations.

Once again, though, we will have to characterize the propositions which make up the codes in the same terms in which we have characterized the ordinary epistemic judgments and this will give rise to the following problems.

First, just as it was hard to see how anyone could accept a set of propositions that he knew to be false, so it is hard to see how anyone could accept a set of propositions he knew to be incomplete. So it is hard to see how to accept the relativist's proposal.

Second, if the propositions that constitute the epistemic system are incomplete, it is very hard to see how they could constitute a conception of anything, let alone a conception of epistemic justification. Before they could be said to amount to a conception of anything, they would have to be completed. But our only idea about how to complete them is by reference to epistemic systems. And now we would seem to have embarked on a vicious regress in which we never succeed in specifying the conception of epistemic justification which is supposed to constitute a particular community's epistemic system.

Third, how are we to understand the phrase 'in relation to epistemic system C'? Since we have said that both the propositions which constitute a system as well as the ordinary epistemic propositions are incomplete, that relation cannot be the relation of logical entailment. 'Relative to epistemic system C', then, must be understood as expressing some non-logical relation that obtains between a belief's being justified and some epistemic system. But what could such a non-logical relation possibly be?

For all of these reasons, then, it looks as though relinquishing the assumption that epistemic systems are made up of complete propositions will not help resuscitate epistemic relativism. Henceforth, then, I shall put it aside.[4]

Epistemic Pluralism

We can approach the incoherence in the epistemic relativist's view from another direction, by looking at his pluralist clause.

---

[4] The problems we have been uncovering for epistemic relativism extend well beyond this particular case. They arise for a relativistic view of any domain which meets the following condition: the parameter to which we are urged to relativize the ordinary, particular judgments of that domain consists of a set of propositions of much the same type as those ordinary judgments. For a discussion of how this affects standard formulations of moral relativism, see my "What is Relativism?" in *Truth and Realism,* ed. M. Lynch and P. Greenough, (Oxford: Oxford University Press, forthcoming).

There are many fundamentally different, genuinely alternative epistemic systems, but no facts by virtue of which one of these systems is more correct than any of the others. (Epistemic pluralism)

Let us begin by asking: does this clause mean to claim that there are many *actual* alternative epistemic systems, or only that there are many *possible* alternative such systems? Since the latter claim is safer (because weaker) let us use it (we shall come back to this issue below).

On this construal, the relativist's thought is that there are many possible alternative epistemic systems, but no facts by virtue of which one of them is more correct than any of the others. But there is a serious puzzle seeing how any such claim could possibly be true.

I am going to grant for the moment that there *may* be different epistemic systems that are genuine alternatives to one another in the sense that they yield *conflicting* verdicts on what it would be justified to believe under specified evidential conditions. (I shall come back to the question whether this is really possible in the next chapter.)

Now, as we have just been emphasizing, an epistemic system consists of a set of normative propositions that specify under what conditions beliefs are and are not justified. So, we will have one system, C_1, which says that:

If E, then belief B is justified

and we will have another system, C_2, which contradicts it and says:

It is not the case that if E, then B is justified.

(The systems of Galileo and Bellarmine illustrate precisely such a conflict.)

In such a circumstance, however, it is very hard to see how the relativist's pluralist clause, which says that all epistemic systems are on a par as far as their correctness is concerned, could possibly be true. For, presumably, either it is the case that E is sufficient for B to be justified, or it is not. If we say, with the relativist, that E is *not* sufficient for B to be justified, because there are no absolute facts about justification, then C1 makes a false assertion; but C2, which denies that E is sufficient for B's justification, then says something *true*. How, then, could it possibly be true to say that there can be no facts by virtue of which some of these systems are more correct than any of the others?

Every epistemic system will have a possible alternative that contradicts it. Take any such contradictory pair. If one of them is deemed to say something false, the other will have to be deemed to have said something true. Under those circumstances, it's hard to see how it could be right to say that there are no facts by virtue of which one epistemic system could be more correct than any other.

Thus, there is also a serious difficulty in seeing how the relativist's pluralist clause could be true.

Epistemic Systems as Sets of Imperatives?

If we think of epistemic systems as composed of propositions, we will have to think of those propositions as complete, truth-evaluable propositions which encode a particular conception of epistemic justification. And if we do that, we will fail to make sense of epistemic relativism. We will be unable to understand how we could coherently accept the relativist's recommendation that we speak not of what is justified and unjustified, but only of what is justified or unjustified relative to the epistemic systems that we happen to accept. For we will no longer be able to make sense of our acceptance of some of those systems over others; and we will no longer be able to make sense of the relativist's pluralist claim that there can be no facts by virtue of which some of those systems are more correct than any of the others.

The question arises whether there is some non-propositional way of making sense of an epistemic system. And in this connection, the most common suggestion is that we think of epistemic systems not as sets of normative propositions, but as sets of *imperatives*—not as *claims* to the effect that E justifies B, but as *commands* of the form: If E, believe B!

This proposal would certainly evade the letter of some of the objections we have been pressing, for those objections depend on construing epistemic systems as sets of general propositions. It is not at all clear, however, that the proposal on offer is workable.

First, ordinary remarks to the effect that some item of information E justifies a particular belief B are not happily taken to be imperatives. An imperative of the form "If E, believe B" *requires* belief B given E, whereas the ordinary remark simply *permits* belief B given E, but does not require it.

Second, we would need some account of what makes any such system of imperatives *epistemic* imperatives, as opposed to *moral* or *pragmatic* imperatives, so that they may be said to embody a conception of *epistemic justification* as opposed to a conception of something else. But no such account has ever been provided and none seems forthcoming.

Finally, it is not easy to see how to make sense of the relativization, on the proposed view of epistemic systems. The idea, recall, is that we should no longer say

1. Copernicanism is justified by Galileo's observations

but only

2. According to the epistemic system that we accept, Science, Copernicanism is justified by Galileo's observations,

where Science is now to be understood as consisting in a set of imperatives of the form:

If E, then believe B.

But what, exactly, does (2) mean, on an imperatival understanding of epistemic systems? What does it mean to say: According to the following system of imperatives, Copernicanism is justified by Galileo's observations?

The only sense of it we can make, I think, is to think of it as offering an analysis of claim (1) in terms of something of the form:

3. According to the system of imperatives that we accept, if certain observations have been made, then believe Copernicanism.

In other words, the only way I can see to make sense of the imperatival construal is to think of it as offering an account of the meaning of such sentences "Copernicanism is justified by Galileo's observations" in terms of facts about which systems of imperatives we accept.

But this proposal would seem to land us right back in the difficulties we uncovered in Chapter 4. The trouble is that a statement like (3) seems to be a purely factual remark about what imperatives we accept and a purely logical remark about what they require. And as we have already seen, it is impossible in this way to capture the normativity of an epistemic remark, a normativity that even a relativist would need to capture.

Conclusion

Rorty says that different communities may operate with different epistemic systems and that there can be no facts by virtue of which one of these systems is any more correct than any of the others. But we have found no way to make sense of this. In particular, we have found no way of construing the notion of an epistemic system so as to render stable a relativistic conception of epistemic justification. The question is where we go from here.[5]

[5] The sort of epistemic relativism we have been considering in this book, in which the relativizing parameter is an epistemic system, is, as we have seen from the discussion of Rorty and Wittgenstein, a classic version of the view. It is possible to imagine other sorts of "epistemic relativism," ones in which we relativize not to a thinker's epistemic system, but rather to his "starting point," to where he finds himself at the start of his reflections. Without being able to go into the matter in the requisite detail, let me briefly indicate why I do not give such alternative versions of epistemic relativism pride of place in this book. The main reason is that a theorist who proposes to relativize facts about justification to a thinker's starting point, rather than to his epistemic system, does not evade a commitment to absolute normative epistemic truths. Rather, what such a theorist would be saying is that the only sorts of absolute epistemic truths there are, are ones which advert to the thinker's starting point. My focus in this book, though, is on the much more radical 'postmodern' view which attempts to evade commitment to any absolute epistemic truths of any kind. Nor is my focus here just a reflection of current fashions; for there is a sense in which the radical view is a much more serious contender than the moderate, absolutist version. It is easy to see what might motivate someone to take seriously the idea that there are *no* absolute epistemic truths of any kind; it is much harder to see what would motivate the moderate view that, while there are some absolute epistemic truths, there are many fewer than we had been inclined to suppose, or that they make essential reference to such parameters as a thinker's starting point. Epistemic truths, after all, are normative truths and it has always seemed hard to understand how normative truths could be built into the impersonal fabric of the universe. Furthermore, there is the epistemic argument that we gave in the previous chapter. Both of these arguments, however, are arguments for *thoroughgoing relativisms* about the epistemic; they are not arguments for the moderate view.

7

The Paradox Resolved

Where Do We Stand?

On the one hand, we have presented a seemingly compelling
argument, based on the inevitable norm-circularity of justifications of our epistemic systems, for a form of relativism about
epistemic judgments. On the other hand, we have seen that such
a relativism is riddled with seemingly insuperable problems.

At this point in the argument, then, we seem perched on the
brink of paradox: we seem to have reason both to accept epistemic relativism and to reject it.

If we are to extricate ourselves from the grip of this conun-
drum, we must show either that a relativism about epistemic
principles is sustainable after all, or that the argument from
norm-circularity never gave it much support to begin with.

I see no hope at all for the first option, but considerable
promise in the second. In the remainder of this chapter, I will
begin the complicated task of explaining why the argument from
norm-circularity should not be credited with supporting epistemic relativism (more precisely, why it should not be seen as
supporting epistemic non-absolutism).

Defusing the Argument from Norm-Circularity

Our argument for Epistemic Relativism depended heavily on the following two claims, which we may now label for convenience:

(7) If there are absolute epistemic facts, it is possible to arrive at justified beliefs about what they are. (Possible)

(8) It is not possible to arrive at justified beliefs about what absolute epistemic facts there are. (Justification)

If epistemic relativism is indeed false, as I have claimed, then one of these premises must be false. In my view, the culprit is Justification: we can arrive at justified beliefs about what absolute epistemic facts there are.

As the reader may recall, we argued for Justification by arguing for a somewhat different claim. Suppose we call our own epistemic system C_1; then the argument we gave for justification was in reality an argument for:

(Encounter) If we were to encounter a fundamental, genuine alternative to our epistemic system, C2, we would not be able to justify C_1 over C2, even by our own lights.

We now face two questions.

(A) How strong was the case for Encounter?

(B) Supposing Encounter was true, how well would it support Justification?

Coherence

Taking the first question first, we surely wouldn't want to say that if we were to encounter *any* fundamentally different, genuine alternative to our epistemic system, we wouldn't be able to justify ours over it. At a minimum, the alternative system would have to be *coherent*, and that is a significant constraint that will weed out many would-be contenders.

There are several different respects in which an epistemic system might fail to be coherent.

First, it is possible for an epistemic system to deliver *inconsistent* verdicts on the question what to believe, so that, with respect to a given evidential situation, it tells us both to believe p and not to believe p. For example, one of the many possible epistemic systems out there is one that incorporates the following epistemic principle:

> If it visually seems to S as though there is a dog in front of him, then it is justified for S to believe that there is a dog in front of him and not justified for S to believe that there is a dog in front of him.

This is obviously an extreme example of an objectively flawed epistemic principle, but it serves to make the important point that we cannot ultimately make sense of the crucial pluralist claim that there are no facts whatsoever which discriminate between all the possible epistemic systems out there.

A somewhat subtler example of an incoherent epistemic system is given by the example of a system which doesn't *overtly* deliver inconsistent verdicts about what to believe but which *entails* such inconsistent verdicts.

Another important sub-class of incoherent epistemic systems consists of those that are not so much internally inconsistent but which prescribe inconsistent beliefs.[1] Once again, it can do so either overtly or by entailing inconsistent beliefs. And once again we have objectively valid reasons, other things being equal, for preferring epistemic systems that do not have this feature.

---

[1] It is true that there are some philosophers who claim that some contradictions can be true and so that we don't always have reason to avoid them. But this is not a widely accepted view.

Furthermore, and as we have previously discussed, an epistemic system can be incoherent in being *self-undermining*, ruling against its own correctness or reliability. Consider, for example, the epistemic principle:

> For all propositions p, it is justified to believe p if and only if the Supreme Court says that p.

If we tried to operate with this principle, we would believe a proposition if and only if the Supreme Court told us to. But if we ask the Supreme Court whether we should believe any factual proposition only if it told us to do so, it would presumably tell us that that would be absurd, that it is only authoritative on questions concerning the US constitution.

Beyond these relatively obvious norms, the requirement of coherence extends considerably further, reaching, for example, to issues concerning the uniformity with which beliefs in various propositions are treated. We have what we might call a *no arbitrary distinctions* principle.

> If an epistemic system (or its user) proposes to treat two propositions p and q according to distinct epistemic principles, it must recognize some epistemically relevant difference between p and q.
>
> If an epistemic system (or its user) proposes to treat two propositions p and q according to the same epistemic principles, it must not recognize any epistemically relevant difference between p and q.

I will not develop these constraints of coherence further, although I believe that there are more of them and that their importance has been underestimated. Each of these norms of coherence can be shown to flow relatively directly from the very *nature* of an epistemic system, as a system of principles that is designed to tell us what there is reason to believe; and I don't think we would so much as understand someone who pretended to believe that incoherence in an epistemic system is a virtue rather than a vice.

At a minimum, then, the most that we could hope to show is not Encounter but rather:

(Encounter*) If we were to encounter a *coherent,* fundamental, genuine alternative to our epistemic system, C2, we would not be able to justify C1 over C2, even by our own lights.

Encounter versus Justification

However, even this seems too strong.

All parties to this dispute should agree that each thinker is *blindly entitled* to his own epistemic system—each thinker is entitled to use the epistemic system he finds himself with, without first having to supply an antecedent justification for the claim that it is the correct system.[2] Perhaps it is overdetermined that the relativist will agree with this. But it is worth emphasizing that even the objectivist must do so, on pain of a debilitating skepticism about epistemic justification: if no one is entitled to use an epistemic system without first justifying it, then no one could be entitled to use an epistemic system, for any attempt by the thinker to justify it will depend on his being entitled to use some epistemic system or other.

There is some disagreement among philosophers about how this blind entitlement to an epistemic system is to be explained and even about whether it requires explanation. But some form of blind (unsupported) entitlement to fundamental parts of one's epistemic system is clearly unavoidable.

Naturally, to say this is not to deny that we might legitimately come to doubt parts of our epistemic system and perhaps even to

[2] For more on the notion of blind entitlement see my "Blind Reasoning," *Proceedings of the Aristotelian Society, Supplementary Volume* 77 (2003): 225–48.

seek to revise them. But in the absence of any such legitimate doubt, it would seem, we are entitled to rely on our epistemic systems.

Now, given this inescapable picture of our relation to our own epistemic system, C_1, it seems quite wrong to claim, as Encounter* does, that if we were confronted by a coherent, fundamental, genuine alternative to our epistemic system, C_2, we would not be able to justify C_1 over C_2, even by our own lights. For wouldn't we reason about the correctness of this alternative system just as we would about any other subject matter, using our own epistemic system? And wouldn't we be perfectly entitled to do so, as we have just been emphasizing? How, then, do we now support the claim that we would not be able to justify C_1 over C_2, even by our own lights?

Where does the pro-relativist argument go wrong? It goes wrong, it seems to me, in relying on an overly general application of Fumerton's claim about norm-circular arguments. Fumerton's claim, that we cannot hope to justify our principles through the use of those very principles, is not true in general; it is true only in the special, albeit important, case where we have *legitimately* come to doubt the correctness of our own principles. In the absence of any legitimate reason to doubt them, though, we would be perfectly entitled to rely on them in justifying our system over theirs, just as we would be entitled to rely on them in reasoning about any other subject matter. However, once we have come legitimately to doubt them, it does seem hard to see what value there would be in using them to show that they pronounce themselves perfectly in order.[3]

It is not entirely out of the question that we should come across an alternative epistemic system that made us doubt the correctness of our own epistemic principles. How would we

---

[3] For further discussion, see my "How are Objective Epistemic Reasons Possible?".

imagine this? Well, we would imagine encountering a different community with what are clearly much more advanced scientific and technological abilities. And yet they deny fundamental aspects of our epistemic system and employ alternative principles.

For this encounter to have the desired effect, this alternative epistemic system would clearly have to be a *real-life* epistemic system, with a proven track record, not just some theoretical possibility. Its *actual* achievements would have to be *impressive* enough to make us legitimately doubt the correctness of our own system.[4] Perhaps if we were ever to undergo such an encounter, then under those conditions we might well be unable to justify C1 over C2.

Once again, though, a qualification appears to be in order:

(Encounter**) If we were to encounter an *actual*, coherent, fundamental, genuine alternative to our epistemic system, C2, whose track record was *impressive* enough to make us doubt the correctness of our own system, C1, we would not be able to justify C1 over C2, even by our own lights.

Now, it's a good question just how impressive the achievements of an alternative epistemic system would have to be before they legitimately made us doubt the correctness of our own system; I won't speculate about that. But however low we set those standards, it is perfectly clear that even if Encounter** were true, it would not support Justification, but only:

(Justification*) If a legitimate doubt were to arise about the correctness of our ordinary epistemic principles, we would not be able to arrive at justified beliefs about their correctness.

And the point is that Justification* is completely consistent with the falsity of Justification: it is compatible with our being justified

---

[4] I am grateful to Roger White for pointing out the need to emphasize this point.

in believing a given proposition under given conditions that there are *other* conditions under which we would not be justified in believing that very same proposition. Hence, the central argument for epistemic relativism does not go through.

The Argument Reformulated?

Can the relativist's argument be reformulated to accommodate these points? Here is the strongest shot at such a reformulation that I can think of.

1. If there are absolutely true epistemic principles, then we know what they are.
2. If a legitimate doubt has arisen about the correctness of our own epistemic principles, we do not know which epistemic principles are objectively true.
3. Legitimate doubt about the correctness of our own epistemic principles has arisen (because we have encountered alternative epistemic systems whose track record is impressive enough to make us doubt ours).

Hence,

4. We do not know which absolute epistemic principles are true.

Hence,

5. There are no absolutely true epistemic principles.

This argument doesn't have anything like the appeal of the original. While it is very plausible to claim that, if there are absolutely correct epistemic principles, they ought to be accessible in principle, it is much less plausible to claim that if there are such principles, we must know what they are here and now, in the actual world.

But even if we were to concede this implausibly demanding first premise, there would still be a problem with this argument—namely, with its third premise.

Up to this point, I have been pretending as though we know of at least two coherent, fundamental competing alternatives to our own epistemic system—namely, those used by Bellarmine and the Azande—that are impressive enough to arouse legitimate doubts in us about the correctness of our own system. But as I shall now try to show, this is completely false.

I will not argue that they are insufficiently impressive to make us doubt the correctness of our system, although that is surely right. What I will argue instead is that in the one case (Bellarmine's) it is not a fundamentally different epistemic system after all, and, in the other (Azande) it is not a competing alternative to ours. By the time we are done, we will be in a position to see that it is much harder than one may be inclined to assume at first blush, to come up with an epistemic system that is a genuine fundamental alternative to the ordinary one.

Bellarmine

Start with Bellarmine. Yes, the Cardinal consults his Bible to find out what to believe about the heavens, rather than using the telescope; but he doesn't divine what the Bible itself contains, but rather reads it using his eyes. Nor does he check it every hour to make sure that it still says the same, but rather relies on induction to predict that it will say the same tomorrow as it does today. And, finally, he uses deductive logic to deduce what it implies about the make-up of the heavens.

For many ordinary propositions, then—propositions about what J. L. Austin called "medium-sized specimens of dry goods"—Bellarmine uses exactly the same epistemic system we use. About the heavens, though, we diverge—we use our eyes, he consults the Bible. Is this really an example of a coherent fundamentally different epistemic system; or is it just an example of someone using the very same epistemic norms we use to arrive at a surprising *theory* about the world—namely, that a certain book, admittedly written many years ago by several different hands, is the revealed word of God and so may *rationally* be taken to be authoritative about the heavens? The question, in other words is, is the principle we dubbed "Revelation" in Chapter 5 an example of a fundamental or merely *derived* epistemic principle?[5]

If Bellarmine's Vatican were to be a genuine example of a coherent fundamentally different epistemic system, he would have to hold that whereas ordinary epistemic principles apply to propositions about objects in his immediate vicinity, Revelation applies to propositions about the heavens. But this would only make sense if he also believed that propositions about the heavens are different in kind from propositions about earthly matters, so that vision might be thought to be an inappropriate means for fixing beliefs about them. But doesn't he use his eyes to note that the sun is shining, or that the moon is half full, or that the clear night-time Roman sky is littered with stars? And doesn't he think that the heavens are in a physical space that is above us, only some distance away? If all this is true, how could he think that observation is not relevant to what we should believe about the heavens, given that he relies on it in everyday life?

On pain of attributing to Bellarmine an incoherent epistemic system, then, we had better regard his system as differing from ours only in some derived sense, attributing to him the view that there is evidence, of a perfectly ordinary sort, that the Holy Scripture is the revealed word of the Creator of the Universe. And it is only natural for someone with that belief to place a

---

[5] (Revelation) For certain propositions p, including propositions about the heavens, believing p is prima facie justified if p is the revealed word of God as claimed by the Bible.

great deal of stock in what it has to say about the heavens—enough, perhaps, to override the evidence provided by observation.

The question then becomes whether there is after all evidence of a perfectly ordinary sort for believing that what was written down in some book by a large number of people over a vast period of time, internal inconsistencies and all, is really the revealed word of the Creator. And that is of course a dispute that we have been having at least since the Enlightenment.

Pace Rorty, then, it is hard to understand the dispute between Galileo and Bellarmine as a dispute between epistemic systems which disagree on the fundamental epistemic principles. It is rather a dispute, within a common epistemic system, as to the origins and nature of the Bible.

Similar remarks apply to the Azande use of an oracle.

The Logic of the Azande

What, though, about the claim that the Azande differ from us in another respect, in their rejection of the principle modus ponens? Unlike Revelation, Modus Ponens has a fair claim to be considered a fundamental epistemic principle, not a derived one.

Recall the Azande belief that only the close paternal kinsmen of a known witch can be counted upon to be witches, whilst also accepting the claim that witchcraft substance is transmitted patrilineally. The contradiction would seem too obvious to miss, if it really were a contradiction. Doesn't that show that the Azande are using a different logic from ours?

Let's look a little more closely. If witchcraft substance is transmitted patrilineally, then every male witch transmits it to all his sons, and they transmit it to all their sons, and so forth. Hence, one incontestable case of witchcraft substance identification looks to be enough to establish that all the males in a given clan are witches. If the Azande refuse to accept this inference, what could explain their reluctance?

The epistemic relativist wants to say that the Azande endorse a different logic, one that doesn't permit the inferences that ours does; but there are at least three other possible explanations of the Azande logical behavior.

First, they might be making a logical mistake, blind to the implications of what they believe. Second, we might be making a mistake in our understanding of them, wrongly translating what they are telling us. Is 'transmitted patrilineally' really the right translation of what they think about the inheritance of witchcraft; is 'if' really the right translation of the logical particle they are using? Perhaps when their thoughts are understood correctly they are not denying anything we assert. Finally, perhaps they are not all that reluctant to accept the inferences we are keen to press on them after all, but simply not that interested in the relevant propositions.

Evans-Pritchard himself seemed to prefer something like the last option. On his view, the Azande's interests tend to be local and specific, as opposed to general or theoretical. It's not that they reject the relevant inferences; they just don't care to go there.

Even if we rejected this explanation, however, there is a very powerful consideration that militates against the relativist option and in favor of the mistranslation option. It derives from reflection on the connection between the meaning of the logical words— 'if', 'and' and 'or' and the like—and the rules for their use.

Let us ask: What conditions must someone satisfy if he is to mean *if* by a given expression—by the English word 'if,' for example? After all, the expression 'if' is just a mark on paper, or a sound in someone's mouth. A parrot could mouth that sound and not mean anything by it. When someone does use it meaningfully, to express the conditional concept *if*, by virtue of what sort of fact does that come about? What is it for someone to use the word 'if' and mean *if* by it?

Extensive reflection on this purely meaning-theoretic question has led many philosophers to favor the following answer: it is by being prepared to use 'if' according to certain rules and not others. It is a difficult question to say in general *which* rules are meaning-constituting in this sense, but the answer in particular cases seems clear. To mean conjunction by 'and', for example, it is necessary and sufficient that a thinker be prepared to use the expression according to the following rules (the so-called standard introduction and elimination rules): From and 'A and B' infer A, from and 'A and B' infer B, and from both A and B, infer 'A and B.' In standard notation:

A and B	A and B	A, B
-----------	------------	------------
A	B	A and B

Similarly, one of the rules that a thinker has to follow in order to mean the conditional concept *if* by 'if' is precisely modus ponens: From A and 'If A, then B', infer B.

P
If P, then Q

Q

If such an inferentialist view of the meaning of the logical constants is correct, however, as many philosophers are inclined to think, then the Azande and we are not really disagreeing about the validity of the rule modus ponens. If the Azande employ different rules for inferences involving 'if,' (or the Azande equivalent) this would simply show that they mean something different by that word than we do by 'if.'

For the Azande to count as employing a genuinely alternative inferential principle to ours, they would have to deny an inference that we affirm, such as the following:

(1) Abu has witchcraft substance

(2) If x has witchcraft substance, then all of x's patrilineal male descendants have witchcraft substance

(3) Julian is one of Abu's patrilineal male descendants

Therefore,

(4) Julian has witchcraft substance

(5) If anyone has witchcraft substance, then that person is a witch

Therefore,

(6) Julian is a witch

If, however, the Azande don't mean what we do by their equivalent of 'if,' then we could not be disagreeing over precisely *this* inference. Just because someone utters the *sentence* 'Pigs can fly,' doesn't necessarily show that he believes something I reject: what if he were using the word 'pig' to mean **bird**?

The intimate relation between the meanings of logical expressions and the inferential rules that govern them makes it difficult to see how we could describe cases where two communities genuinely disagree about which inferential rules are correct. The connection will make it seem as though there is no real disagreement, just a choice of different concepts.

In trying to describe radically alternative practices of inferring and counting, Wittgenstein was constantly running into trouble with this point. In his *Remarks on the Foundations of Mathematics*, for example, he attempts to describe a community of people who sell wood at a price proportionate to the area covered by the wood rather than, as we would do it, at a price proportionate to the cubic measure of the wood. He suggests that attempts to persuade them that area is an inadequate measure of quantity may not succeed:

How could I show them that—as I should say—you don't really buy more wood if you buy a pile covering a bigger area?—I should, for instance, take a pile which was small by their ideas, and, by laying the logs around, change it into a 'big' one. This *might* convince them—but perhaps they would say: "Yes, now it's a *lot* of wood and costs more"—and that would be the end of the matter.[6]

But think of all the other things these people would have to believe, if they are to make coherent sense of their practice.[7] They would have to believe that a two-by-four inch board suddenly increased in size or quantity when it was turned from resting on its two-inch side to resting on its four-inch side; that more wood doesn't necessarily mean more weight; that people shrink when they shift from standing on both legs to standing on one; that a quantity of wood was adequate for building a given house when it was in the lumber yard, but not now that it has been brought to the empty lot and stacked neatly in the corner.

Surely, it is far more plausible that these people mean something different by 'more' and by 'cost' than we do, as Wittgenstein in effect acknowledges:

We should presumably say in this case: they simply do not mean the same by "a lot of wood" and "a little wood" as we do; and they have quite a different system of payment from us.[8]

If that is right, however, they may not be denying anything that we regard as obviously true and the attempt to describe a genuine alternative to our epistemic system will have failed once again.

Conclusion

Many influential thinkers—Wittgenstein and Rorty included—have suggested that there are powerful considerations in favor of

[6] Ludwig Wittgenstein, *Remarks on the Foundations of Mathematics*, rev. edn., ed. G. H. von Wright, R. Rhees and G. E. M. Anscombe, trans. G. E. M. Anscombe (Cambridge, Mass.: The MIT Press, 1978), part I, para. 150.

[7] See Barry Stroud, "Wittgenstein and Logical Necessity," in his *Meaning, Understanding and Practice: Philosophical Essays* (Oxford: Oxford University Press, 2000), 1–16.

[8] Wittgenstein, *Remarks on the Foundations of Mathematics*, part I, para. 150.

a relativistic view of epistemic judgments, arguments which draw on the alleged existence of alternative epistemic systems and the inevitable norm-circularity of any justification we might offer for our own epistemic systems. Although such arguments may seem initially seductive, they do not ultimately withstand critical scrutiny. Moreover, there are decisive objections to epistemic relativism. It would seem, then, that we have no option but to think that there are absolute, practice-independent facts about what beliefs it would be most reasonable to have under fixed evidential conditions.

It remains a question of considerable importance—and contemporary interest—whether, given a person's evidence, the epistemic facts always dictate a *unique* answer to the question what is to be believed or whether there are cases in which they permit some rational disagreement.[9] So there is a question about the *extent* of the epistemic objectivism to which we are committed. But it looks as though we have every reason to believe that some version or other of such an objectivist view will be sustainable without fear of paradox.

[9] See Roger White, "Epistemic Permissiveness," *Philosophical Perspectives* (forthcoming).

8

Epistemic Reasons and the Explanation of Belief

Believing for Reasons

In the preceding chapters, I argued that facts about what belief would be justified by a given piece of evidence are facts that must be thought of as absolute, and not as varying from social context to social context. Interesting as this claim about justification may be, it wouldn't matter very much if it weren't possible for us to be *moved* to belief *by* our epistemic reasons. For as we saw in Chapter 2, a potent form of a constructivism about knowledge can assume the form of a:

> *Constructivism about Rational Explanation:* It is never possible to explain why we believe what we believe solely on the basis of our exposure to the relevant evidence: our contingent needs and interests must also be invoked.

Now, there is a danger that this thesis will be heard as making less of a point than is intended. In most cases, it goes without saying that our exposure to the relevant evidence will not suffice to explain why we form the beliefs that we form. In addition to exposure to the relevant evidence, we would need to have an interest in the question at issue, the conceptual apparatus with which to grasp the evidence and the raw intelligence to compute its relevance. The constructivist about rational explanation is not after these timid and obvious points, and henceforth I shall take them for granted. The constructivist's claim, rather, is that even after all these factors have been taken into account, exposure to the relevant evidence can still never suffice to explain why we form the beliefs that we form.

How might it come about that our exposure to the evidence never suffices to explain why we believe what we believe, that our contingent social interests must always play an ineliminable role?

There look to be two ways: either because our epistemic reasons never make *any* contribution whatsoever to the causal explanation of our beliefs, so that the correct explanation is always exclusively in terms of our social interests; or because, less radically, although our epistemic reasons do make some contribution, they can never be adequate by themselves to explain our beliefs and contingent social interests are needed to take up the slack.

Let us call the first thesis strong constructivism about rational explanation and the second one weak constructivism about rational explanation. I shall examine each thesis in turn.

Strong Constructivism: The Symmetry Principles

Let me say straight away that it is impossible for me to see how strong constructivism could be true. There are undoubtedly some beliefs which need to be explained exclusively in terms of social factors rather than evidential ones. If we ask why Christianity is so widely believed in the American South but not in Iran, the explanation would surely not be in terms of the differing evidence available in America and Iran as to the credibility of the claims made in the Christian Bible. Rather, the correct explanation would appeal to the different religious traditions that have developed in the two regions and to the interests that people have in conforming to local practices.

But it is very difficult to see what could justify generalizing this style of explanation to all beliefs. After all, the epistemic reasons for a belief are either experiences, or other beliefs, bearing an appropriate justificatory relation to it. What could prevent such items from *causing* that belief on certain occasions? Couldn't my seeming to see the cat on the roof fully explain why I believe that the cat is on the roof on some occasion?

Strong constructivism originates in one of the founding texts of the literature that has come to be known as "the sociology of scientific knowledge" (SSK)—David Bloor's *Knowledge and Social Imagery*.[1] As far as I can tell, the main explanation for why it has appealed to so many scholars is that it came to be conflated with a different thesis, one that is much more plausible.

The history and the sociology of science has long been an important area of research. Science is a complex social enterprise and there is clearly considerable scope for studying its socio-logical and political aspects in a rigorous and responsible manner. Central questions might include: How are the institutions of science organized? How is power distributed? What proportion of social wealth is devoted to scientific study and how is that funding distributed? What review and evaluation procedures are employed? And so forth.

What distinguishes SSK from the history and sociology of science more traditionally conceived is the ambition not merely to describe the institutions of science but to explain the very *content* of scientific theories. As Bloor put it:

---

[1] Bloor, *Knowledge and Social Imagery*, 1st edn. Other prominent texts in this tradition include Bruno Latour and Steve Woolgar, *Laboratory Life: The Social Construction of Scientific Facts* (Beverly Hills, Calif.: Sage Publications, 1979), and Andrew Pickering, *Constructing Quarks: A Sociological History of Particle Physics* (Chicago: University of Chicago Press, 1984).

Can the sociology of knowledge investigate and explain the very content and nature of scientific knowledge? Many sociologists believe that it cannot. They say that knowledge as such, as distinct from the circumstances surrounding its production, is beyond their grasp. They voluntarily limit the scope of their own enquiries. I shall argue that this is a betrayal of their disciplinary standpoint.[2]

Bloor goes on to say that by "knowledge" he doesn't mean justified true belief but rather "those beliefs which people confidently hold to and live by," what people "take to be knowledge." In other words, the discipline he is proposing would seek to explain why certain propositions come to be widely believed to be true.

In defining the methodology of this new discipline, Bloor wrote:

1 It would be causal, that is, concerned with the conditions which bring about belief or states of knowledge.
2 It would be impartial with respect to truth or falsity, rationality or irrationality, success or failure.
3 It would be symmetrical in its style of explanation ....The symmetry postulate ... enjoins us to seek the same kind of causes for both true and false, [and] rational and irrational, beliefs...[3]

Although they are often mentioned in the same breath, there is all the difference in the world between a symmetry postulate concerning truth and one concerning rationality. One can make a semi-plausible case for a symmetry principle about truth, but that would do nothing to further strong constructivism, since one way to explain both true and false beliefs through the same kind of cause is to explain each of them *evidentially*.

On the other hand, the symmetry principle concerning rationality does entail strong constructivism, since the only way to ensure that both rational and irrational beliefs are explained through the

[2] Bloor, *Knowledge and Social Imagery*, 2nd edn., 3.
[3] ibid. 7 and 175.

same kind of cause is to explain both of them non-evidentially. But there is not even a semi-plausible case to be made for it.

Symmetry about Truth

Here is the semi-plausible case that we can make for symmetry about truth.[4] Suppose we are trying to explain why, prior to Aristotle, people believed that the earth was flat. Well, it seems flat, at least when taken in the small. Given the size of the earth, local patches of it appear flat; its curvature only becomes visually apparent when it is viewed from a height above the earth's surface.

It took some subtle reasoning on Aristotle's part to reveal that a flat earth could not explain the known astronomical facts. For example, Aristotle pointed out, during a lunar eclipse the shape of earth's shadow seen on the moon is always round, an effect that would be produced only by a spherical object. If the earth were a flat disk, there would be some occasions when the sunlight would strike the disk edge on, resulting in a shadow that would look more like a line. Furthermore, as a traveler heads either north or south, stars that are not visible at home are seen to rise above the horizon and move across the sky suggesting that the traveler must have moved across a curved surface.[5]

Pre-Aristotelian Greeks believed falsely that the earth is flat; we believe truly that it is round. Nevertheless, the explanation

---

[4] I am setting aside, for the sake of argument, the important objection that the proffered theses are impossibly vague, because we have not been told what it would be for two explanations to invoke or fail to invoke the same "types" of cause.

[5] See Aristotle, *On the Heavens*, trans by W. K. C. Guthrie (Cambridge, Mass.: Harvard University Press, 1939).

for each of our beliefs looks to invoke causes "of the same type,"—in terms of the evidence available for those beliefs. Since, as we pointed out in Chapter 2, evidence is *fallible*, it is entirely consistent with a belief's falsity that it is explainable through evidential causes.

The case is only semi-plausible because it is doubtful that *all* belief can be treated symmetrically with respect to truth. Some propositions are so obvious that it would be difficult to explain belief in them in terms of the very same causes that explain belief in their negations. Virtually all of us would agree that red looks a lot more like orange than it looks like blue. Suppose you came across someone who denied this. It wouldn't be tempting to try to explain this person's belief in terms of the impoverished evidence available to them about how the colors look. Either you know how red, orange and blue look or you don't. Rather, the suspicion would arise that such a person suffered from a sort of color blindness, or meant something different by at least one of the ingredient color terms. Our reaction to the belief would be controlled by the thought: "If this were the belief it would be obviously false, so it must be some other belief after all." A stance of neutrality about the truth or falsity of the belief would yield, in all likelihood, an incorrect explanation of its genesis.

We may put it this way. Not every belief needs to be supported by some independent item of information that would constitute evidence in its favor: some beliefs are *intrinsically* credible or self-evident. Philosophers disagree about the range of propositions that they think are self-evident in this sense, and very few believe that their number is large. But ever since Descartes first formulated his famous *cogito* argument, philosophers have been persuaded that at least some propositions are self-evident. What non-circular evidence could one adduce, for example, for the belief that one is currently conscious?[6]

Symmetry about Rationality

So it is doubtful that, at least with respect to highly obvious propositions, the symmetry principle concerning truth holds.

For present purposes, however, I propose to grant it. Let us assume henceforth that there are no self-evident beliefs.

This concession by itself does nothing for strong constructivism because strong constructivism requires symmetry about rationality and that thesis is in no way supported by symmetry about truth. On the contrary, our case for the truth principle rested on the *falsity* of the principle about rationality because it leaned on our being able to explain both true and false beliefs evidentially.

Not only do we lack any good argument for strong constructivism, we would appear to possess a number of powerful considerations against it.

First, and as I previously mentioned, it is impossible to see what would prevent our epistemic reasons from sometimes causing our beliefs. Our epistemic reasons are just experiences and thoughts that bear an appropriate justificatory relationship to our beliefs. What could possibly stop them from occasionally causing those beliefs?

Second, we need to be able to make a distinction between a belief that is to be commended for being appropriately grounded in a consideration which justifies it, versus one that is to be criticized as merely grounded in prejudice. But as John Dupré has rightly pointed out, that sort of distinction would be rendered impossible by a symmetry principle about rationality:

---

[6] An example I have often heard from Stephen Schiffer.

By asserting that all scientific belief should be explained in terms of the goals, interests, and prejudices of the scientist, and denying any role whatever for the recalcitrance of nature, it leaves no space for the criticism of specific scientific beliefs on the grounds that they do reflect such prejudices rather than being plausibly grounded in fact.[7]

Finally, and relatedly, there is a looming problem with self-refutation. Wouldn't anyone promoting the view that epistemic reasons never move people to belief need to represent himself as having come to *that* view precisely *because* it is justified by the appropriate considerations?

Strong constructivism about rational explanation, then, seems wrong, unwarranted and unstable.

The Underdetermination of Belief by Evidence: Thomas Kuhn

By contrast, the weak constructivist thesis about rational explanation seems initially, far more plausible. According to this thesis, although evidence can enter into the explanation of belief, it is never *enough* to explain it because any evidence we might possess necessarily *underdetermines* the specific belief that we arrive at on its basis.

This idea, that the evidence in science always underdetermines the theories that we believe on its basis, has exerted considerable influence in the philosophy of science, even in non-constructivist circles. What is the view and how is it motivated? There are two important sources for the view, the first empirical and historical and the second a priori and philosophical.

The first derives from Thomas Kuhn's enormously influential work on the history of science. On Kuhn's picture, much of what

---

[7] John Dupré, *The Disorder of Things: Metaphysical Foundations of the Disunity of Science* (Cambridge, Mass.: Harvard University Press, 1993), 12–13.

passes for science is "normal science." Normal science consists essentially of puzzle solving. Against the backdrop of an assumed set of questions concerning a particular domain—the heavens, for example, or the nature of combustion—and a set of standards and methods for answering them—scientists attempt to make relatively small changes to the dominant theory of that domain so as to resolve the anomalies that experiment reveals. Kuhn called the set of assumed background questions, standards and methods a 'paradigm.' Notice that a paradigm in this sense *includes* what I have been calling an epistemic system, but goes beyond it: it comprises not only principles of reasoning strictly so-called, but also assumptions about what questions need to be answered and some sense of what would count as a good answer to them. (Kuhn is maddeningly inexplicit about exactly what he takes paradigms to contain; one scholar has counted twenty-two different characterizations in *The Structure of Scientific Revolutions* alone.)

According to Kuhn, every so often the difficulties for the dominant theory accumulate to the point where scientists are forced to reconsider some fundamental assumption that had up to then seemed obvious. Such changes—when one background 'paradigm' gives way to another—Kuhn called "scientific revolutions." Central examples of scientific revolutions include the victory of the Copernican heliocentric system over that of the Ptolemaic; Newton's displacement of Aristotelian theories of motion; and the replacement of Newtonian mechanics by Einsteinian relativity theory, with its attendant reconceptualization of the notions of space and time.

Having established this distinction between normal and revolutionary science, Kuhn proceeded to make a large number of provocative claims about such revolutions based, as he saw it, on a close study of their historical setting. For our purposes, the most important of these claims is this: although we tend to think of these revolutionary changes in paradigm as among the greatest accomplishments of the human intellect, there can be no intelligible sense in which they could be said to have resulted in *better* theories than the ones they replaced, for it is impossible meaningfully to *compare* the pre-revolutionary theories with their post-revolutionary counterparts. Kuhn identified three important sources for such inter-paradigm "incommensurability."

First, he claimed, incommensurability results from the fact that the proponents of competing paradigms often disagree about the list of problems that need to be solved. "Their standards or their definitions of science are not the same."[8] In typical paradigm changes, Kuhn maintained, there will be gains as well as losses and there is no neutral way of deciding whether the gains outweigh the losses.

Second, the newer paradigm will be couched in terms of concepts that proponents of the older paradigm will not be able to express in their language:

Consider ... the men who called Copernicus mad because he proclaimed that the earth moved. They were not either just wrong or quite wrong. Part of what they meant by 'earth' was fixed position. Their earth, at least, could not be moved. Correspondingly, Copernicus' innovation was not simply to move the earth. Rather, it was a whole new way of regarding the problems of physics and astronomy, one that necessarily changed the meaning of both 'earth' and 'motion.' Without those changes, the concept of a moving earth was mad. [9]

Finally, Kuhn concluded, not only do proponents of distinct paradigms speak different languages; there is an important sense in which they don't even live in the same world:

These examples point to the third and most fundamental aspect of the incommensurability of competing paradigms. In a sense that I am unable to explicate further, the proponents of competing paradigms

---

[8] Thomas Kuhn, *The Structure of Scientific Revolutions*, 2nd edn. (Chicago: University of Chicago Press, 1970), 148.

[9] ibid. 149–50.

practice their trades in different worlds. One contains constrained bodies that fall slowly, the other pendulums that repeat their motions over and over again . . . One is embedded in a flat, the other in a curved, matrix of space. Practicing in different worlds, the two groups of scientists see different things when they look from the same point in the same direction.[10]

From all this, Kuhn drew the inevitable conclusion. If scientists subscribing to distinct paradigms "live in different worlds," then it is indeed hard to see how paradigm change could be a rational process:

Just because it is a transition between incommensurables, the transition between competing paradigms cannot be made one step at a time, forced by logic and neutral experience. Like the gestalt switch, it must occur all at once (though not necessarily in an instant) or not at all . . . I would argue . . . that in these matters neither proof nor error is at issue. The transfer of allegiance from paradigm to paradigm is a conversion experience that cannot be forced.[11]

If reasons for thinking that the newer paradigm is closer to the truth are not the causes of paradigm change, what explains how they occur in the first place? What propels a scientist to shift his allegiance from one theory to another one not even comparable with it?

Part of the answer, says Kuhn, is that they very often don't make the transition at all, clinging obstinately to an older paradigm well after the rest of the scientific community had abandoned it. And on those rare occasions when they do shift allegiance, the causes may have to do with a variety of different motives:

Individual scientists embrace a new paradigm for all sorts of reasons and usually for several at once. Some of these reasons—for example, the sun worship that helped make Kepler a Copernican—lie outside the

[10] Ibid. 150.
[11] ibid. 150–1.

apparent sphere of science entirely. Others must depend upon idiosyncrasies of autobiography or personality. Even the nationality or the prior reputation of the innovator and his teachers sometimes play a crucial role.[12]

Kuhn quotes from Max Planck's *Scientific Autobiography* in which the distinguished quantum theorist observed:

A new scientific truth does not triumph by convincing its opponents and making them see the light, but rather because its opponents eventually die, and a new generation grows up that is familiar with it.[13]

Kuhn hastens to add that, just because paradigm change does not admit of justification does not mean that arguments are irrelevant. He concedes that the most common claim made by advocates of a new paradigm is an ability to solve the problems that caused a crisis for the previous paradigm. But he insists that such claims are rarely sufficient by themselves, and nor are they always legitimate. Kuhn concludes:

But paradigm debates are not really about relative problem solving ability, though for good reasons they are usually couched in those terms. Instead, the issue is which paradigm should in the future guide research on problems many of which neither competitor can yet claim to resolve completely. A decision between alternate ways of practicing science is called for, and in the circumstances that decision must be based less on past achievement than on future promise . . . A decision of that kind can only be made on faith . . . Though the historian can always find men—Priestley for instance— who were unreasonable to resist for as long as they did, he will not find a point at which resistance becomes illogical or unscientific. At most he may wish to say that the man who continues to resist after his whole profession has converted has *ipso facto* ceased to be a scientist.[14]

[12] ibid. 153.
[13] ibid. 151.
[14] ibid. 157–8.

Assessing Kuhn's Picture

If Kuhn's claims about incommensurability were right, what would follow? Not weak constructivism, for two reasons. First, there is a problem seeing how an empirical thesis such as Kuhn's could ground a modally characterized thesis like weak constructivism, according to which, *necessarily,* our evidence always falls short of belief. Second, and even if we put this point to one side, it wouldn't follow that *none* of our beliefs can be explained purely evidentially. The most that one could hope to establish with the sort of empirical study of the history of science that Kuhn conducts is a much weaker thesis to the effect that sometimes—or at important junctures—or very often—in the history of science, our evidence has fallen short of what we have ended up believing. And that is a very different proposition from the one that we are being invited to accept.

Still, even this highly qualified thesis would clearly be very important and so it is significant that there are problems with Kuhn's argument even after these qualifications are entered.

To begin first with the most extreme of his claims, there is no plausible sense in which Bellarmine and Galileo lived in "different worlds." If they were talking to each other in the same room then they lived in the same world, in just about any relevant sense of "world." Of course, they believed different propositions about this world; that much is given. But to talk about them living in different worlds is to succumb to the temptation, admittedly ubiquitous in the constructivist literature, to conflate a difference in representation with a difference in the thing represented.

If talk of different worlds is indefensible rhetorical excess, what about the more sober-sounding claims regarding incommensurability? Incommensurability may be divided into two separate issues, one concerning issues of *translation* between theories belonging to competing paradigms and one concerning the standards governing those theories.

Let us say that two theories, T1 and T2, are "conceptually incommensurable" if neither theory can be translated into the other. Notice that to say that T2 and T1 are not intertranslatable is not to claim that no one person could understand both theories: if it did, claims of conceptual incommensurability would be immediately falsified, since it is obvious that Einstein understood both Newtonian mechanics and relativity theory. The claim, rather, is that it is not possible to express the characteristic propositions of T2 in the vocabulary of T1.

Now, failure of translation can occur in one of two ways—it can either be *partial* or it can be *global*. In a global failure, absolutely no proposition of T2 is expressible in T1 and vice versa; in a partial failure, only some claims would fail to translate.

If paradigm changes exhibited global failures of translation, then it would be impossible to see how paradigm change could be a rational process; for if the failure were global, it wouldn't even be possible to determine whether there is any proposition on which the two theories disagree. And in that case it would be impossible to see how one could rationally prefer one theory to the other.

However, partial failure of translation is not necessarily incompatible with paradigm change being rational since all that the latter requires is that it be possible to meaningfully compare at least some of the central claims of the competing theories.

But not even Kuhn denies that one paradigm often replaces another by doing better at solving the problems that caused the crisis for the previous theory. What he says is that such claims are often insufficient by themselves to explain paradigm change, and are sometimes, in addition, "illegitimate," in the sense that the superiority of the new paradigm with respect to those problems is exaggerated by its proponents. But he doesn't say—at least when he is being careful—that they are unintelligible. So, global translation failure is out of the question.

And he himself supplies many compelling examples of shared predictions that provided a basis on which to prefer rationally one theory to the other. For example, even if we were to concede that the Ptolemaic and Copernican paradigms meant different things by 'planet,' 'star' and so forth, there are clearly a number of predictions made by each theory that can be expressed in a neutral language and which the Copernican theory does better at than the Ptolemaic. For example: That thing over there, which we call a 'moon', is more like the earth than it is like a hole in a celestial sphere. Or: There are many more of those things that we all agree in calling 'stars' than is predicted by your theory. And so forth.

These sorts of examples—and Kuhn himself supplies many of them—also cast doubt on the suggestion that competing paradigms cannot meaningfully be compared because they typically differ in the sorts of standards that they bring to bear on the resolution of scientific problems. The problem here is that in many of the cases actually described by Kuhn, there is no discernible disagreement about standards, just a disagreement about predictions.

Its considerable influence on constructivist thought notwithstanding, it is hard to extract from Kuhn's writings a persuasive argument for weak constructivism.

Underdetermination: Duhem on Auxiliary Hypotheses

Some philosophers have thought that such an argument may be found instead in the thought of the turn of the (twentieth) century French physicist and philosopher, Pierre Duhem.

Suppose that an experimental observation is inconsistent with a theory that you believe: the theory predicts that the needle will read '10' and the needle does not budge from zero, say. What Duhem pointed out is that this does not necessarily refute the theory. For the observational prediction is generated not merely on the basis of the theory, but, in addition, through the use of auxiliary hypotheses about the initial conditions of the experimental setup, the functioning of the experimental apparatus and possibly many other claims. In light of the recalcitrant observational result, *something* has to be revised, but so far we do not yet know exactly what: perhaps it's the theory, perhaps it's the auxiliary hypotheses. Perhaps, indeed, it is the very claim that we recorded a genuinely recalcitrant result, as opposed to merely suffering some visual illusion.

Duhem argued that reason alone could never decide which revisions are called for and, hence, that belief revision in science could not be a purely rational matter: something else had to be at work as well. What the social constructivist adds is that this extra element is something social.

It is common to see references to the "Quine–Duhem" thesis of the underdetermination of theory by evidence, thereby linking the thought of the French physicist to that of the recently deceased Harvard philosopher of language, logic and science, Willard van Orman Quine. But Quine never endorsed the view that reason alone cannot tell us which revisions to make in the face of recalcitrant experience. His was the much more limited claim that any evidence we might collect for a given generalization is *logically* consistent with the falsity of that claim.

Quine's observation occurs in the context of a debate about the meaning of theoretical statements in science, not one concerning the rationality of belief revision. The logical positivists had maintained that theoretical statements in the sciences—about electrons, positrons and the like—could be identified with statements about the contents of possible experience. As Quine and a number of other philosophers subsequently showed, however, statements about unobservables always outrun what one can capture in purely observational terms, so that any experiences one might have would be logically consistent with the falsity of any given theoretical statement.

This claim about meaning, however, implies nothing at all about whether some changes to scientific belief are more reasonable than others in the face of recalcitrant experience. As Ian Hacking rightly notes, Quine's point is merely logical: the evidence is formally consistent with more than one theory. That isn't the same as saying that it is *rationally* compatible with more than one theory.[15]

Thomas Nagel has put the point vividly and amusingly:

Suppose I have the theory that a diet of hot fudge sundaes will enable me to lose a pound a day. If I eat only hot fudge sundaes and weigh myself every morning, my interpretation of the numbers on the scale is certainly dependent on a theory of mechanics that explains how the scale will respond when objects of different weights are placed on it. But it is not dependent on my dietary theories. If I concluded from the fact that the numbers keep getting higher that my intake of ice cream must be altering the laws of mechanics in my bathroom, it would be philosophical idiocy to defend the inference by appealing to Quine's dictum that all our statements about the external world face experience as a corporate body, rather than one by one. Certain revisions in response to the evidence are reasonable; others are pathological.[16]

If, however, we cannot appeal to Quine's merely logical point, how should we defend the view that evidence always underdetermines belief? The answer, I believe, is that we can't.

Consider Duhem's example of an astronomer peering through his telescope at the heavens and being surprised at what he finds there, perhaps a hitherto undetected star in a galaxy he has been charting. Upon this discovery, according to Duhem, the astronomer may revise his theory of the heavens or he may revise his theory of how the telescope works. And, according to Duhem, rational principles of belief fixation do not tell him which to do.

---

[15] Hacking, *The Social Construction of What?*, 73
[16] Thomas Nagel, "The Sleep of Reason," *The New Republic*, October 12, 1998, 35.

The idea, however, that in peering at the heavens through a telescope we are testing our theory of the telescope *just as much* as we are testing our astronomical views is absurd. The theory of the telescope has been established by numerous terrestrial experiments and fits in with an enormous number of other things that we know about lenses, light and mirrors. It is simply not plausible that, in coming across an unexpected observation of the heavens, a rational response might be to revise what we know about telescopes. The point is not that we might *never* have occasion to revise our theory of telescopes; one can certainly imagine circumstances under which that is precisely what would be called for. The point is that not *every* circumstance in which something about telescopes is presupposed is a circumstance in which our theory of telescopes is being tested, and so the conclusion that rational considerations alone cannot decide how to respond to recalcitrant experience is blocked.[17]

Conclusion

We have examined three distinct arguments for the claim that we can never explain belief by appeal to our epistemic reasons alone; and we have found grounds for rejecting each and every one of them.

[17] Naturally, many difficult issues about how to understand the confirmation relation remain. For further discussion see Ronald Giere, *Understanding Scientific Reasoning* (New York: Holt, Reinhart and Winston, 1984) and Clark Glymour, *Theory and Evidence* (Princeton: Princeton University Press, 1980).

9
Epilogue

THE core constructivist conviction that we have been concerned with in this book is that knowledge is constructed by societies in ways that reflect their contingent social needs and interests. We have isolated three distinct ideas that this conviction might interestingly amount to and we have examined the case that can be made for them.

On the negative side, there look to be severe objections to each and every version of a constructivism about knowledge that we have examined. A constructivism about truth is incoherent. A constructivism about justification is scarcely any better. And there seem to be decisive objections to the idea that we cannot explain belief through epistemic reasons alone.

On the positive side, we failed to find any good arguments for constructivist views. In the case of a relativism about justification, what appears initially to be a seductive argument fails to hold up under scrutiny.

At its best—for instance, in the work of Simone de Beauvoir and Anthony Appiah[1]—social constructivist thought exposes the contingency of those of our social practices which we had

---

[1] See Simone de Beauvoir, *The Second Sex*, trans. and ed. H. M. Parshley (New York: Knopf, 1953) and K. Anthony Appiah and Amy Gutman, *Color Conscious: The Political Morality of Race* (Princeton: Princeton University Press, 1996).

wrongly come to regard as naturally mandated. It does so by relying on the standard canons of good scientific reasoning. It goes astray when it aspires to become a general theory of truth or knowledge. The difficulty lies in understanding why such generalized applications of social construction have come to tempt so many.

One source of their appeal is clear: they are hugely empowering. If we can be said to know up front that any item of knowledge only has that status because it gets a nod from our contingent social values, then any claim to knowledge can be dispatched if we happen not to share the values on which it allegedly depends.

But that only postpones the real question. Why this fear of knowledge? Whence this felt need to protect against its deliverances?

In the United States, constructivist views of knowledge are closely linked to such progressive movements as post-colonialism and multiculturalism because they supply the philosophical resources with which to protect oppressed cultures from the charge of holding false or unjustified views.

Even on purely political grounds, however, it is difficult to understand how this could have come to seem a good application of constructivist thought: for if the powerful can't criticize the oppressed, because the central epistemological categories are inexorably tied to particular perspectives, it also follows that the oppressed can't criticize the powerful. The only remedy, so far as I can see, for what threatens to be a strongly conservative upshot, is to accept an overt double standard: allow a questionable idea to be criticized if it is held by those in a position of power—Christian creationism, for example—but not if it is held by those whom the powerful oppress—Zuni creationism, for example.

The intuitive view is that there is a way things are that is independent of human opinion, and that we are capable of arriving at belief about how things are that is objectively reason-able, binding on anyone capable of appreciating the relevant evidence regardless of their social or cultural perspective. Difficult as these notions may be, it is a mistake to think that recent philosophy has uncovered powerful reasons for rejecting them.

BIBLIOGRAPHY

Appiah, K. Anthony and Amy Gutman. *Color Conscious: The Political Morality of Race*. Princeton: Princeton University Press, 1996.

Aristotle, *On the Heavens*, translated by W. K. C. Guthrie. Cambridge: Cambridge University Press, 1939.

Barnes, Barry and David Bloor. "Relativism, Rationalism and the Sociology of Knowledge." In *Rationality and Relativism*, ed. Martin Hollis and Steven Lukes, 21–46. Cambridge, Mass.: The MIT Press, 1982.

Bloor, David. *Knowledge and Social Imagery*, 1st edn. London: Routledge & Kegan Paul, 1976; 2nd edn., Chicago: University of Chicago Press, 1991.

Boghossian, Paul. "What the Sokal Hoax Ought to Teach Us." *Times Literary Supplement*, December 13, 1996, 14–15.

—— "How are Objective Epistemic Reasons Possible?" *Philosophical Studies* 106 (2001): 1–40.

—— "Blind Reasoning." *Proceedings of the Aristotelian Society, Supplementary Volume 77* (2003): 225–48.

—— "What is Relativism?" In *Truth and Realism*, ed. M. Lynch and P. Greenough. Oxford: Oxford University Press, forthcoming.

Chabon, Michael. *The Amazing Adventures of Kavalier and Clay*. New York: Picador USA, 2000.

Cohen, Paul. *Set Theory and the Continuum Hypothesis*. New York: W. A. Benjamin, 1966.

de Beauvoir, Simone. *The Second Sex*, trans. and ed. H. M. Parshley. New York: Knopf, 1953.

de Santillana, Giorgio. *The Crime of Galileo*. Chicago: University of Chicago Press, 1955.

Dupré, John. *The Disorder of Things: Metaphysical Foundations of the Disunity of Science*. Cambridge, Mass.: Harvard University Press, 1993.

Evans-Pritchard, E. E. *Witchcraft, Oracles and Magic among the Azande*. Oxford: Clarendon Press, 1937.

Feyerabend, Paul. *Against Method*, 3rd edn. New York: Verso, 1993.

Foucault, Michael. *The History of Sexuality, Volume 1: An Introduction*, trans. from the French by Robert Hurley. New York: Pantheon Books, 1978.

Frazer, James G. *The Golden Bough: A Study in Magic and Religion*, 3 edn., reprint of the 1911 edn. New York: Macmillan, 1980.

Fumerton, Richard. *Metaepistemology and Skepticism*. Lanham, Md.: Rowman & Littlefield, 1995.

Gettier, Edmund. "Is Justified True Belief Knowledge?" *Analysis* 23 (1963): 121–3.

Gibbard, Allan. *Wise Choices, Apt Feelings: A Theory of Normative Judgement*. Cambridge, Mass.: Harvard University Press, 1990.

Giere, Ronald. *Understanding Scientific Reasoning*, 2nd edn. New York: Holt, Reinhart and Winston, 1984.

Glymour, Clark. *Theory and Evidence*. Princeton: Princeton University Press, 1980.

Goodman, Nelson. *Ways of Worldmaking*. Indianapolis: Hackett Publishing Co., 1978.

—— "Notes on the Well-Made World." In *Starmaking: Realism, Anti-Realism, and Irrealism*, ed. Peter McCormick, 151–60. Cambridge, Mass.: The MIT Press, 1996.

Hacking, Ian. *The Social Construction of What?* Cambridge, Mass.: Harvard University Press, 1999.

Harman, Gilbert. *Change in View: Principles of Reasoning*. Cambridge, Mass.: MIT Press, 1986.

—— "Rationality." In his *Reasoning, Meaning, and Mind*, 9–45. Oxford: Clarendon Press, 1999.

—— and Judith Jarvis Thomson. *Moral Relativism and Moral Objectivity.* Cambridge, Mass.: Blackwell Publishers, 1996.

Herrnstein Smith, Barbara. "Cutting-Edge Equivocation: Conceptual Moves and Rhetorical Strategies in Contemporary Anti-Epistemology." *South Atlantic Quarterly* 101, no. 1 (2002): 187–212.

Kant, Immanuel. *Critique of Pure Reason,* trans. Norman Kemp Smith. New York: Macmillan, 1929.

Korsgaard, Christine. *The Sources of Normativity.* Cambridge: Cambridge University Press, 1996.

Kripke, Saul. *Naming and Necessity,* Cambridge, Mass.: Harvard University Press, 1980.

Kuhn, Thomas. *The Structure of Scientific Revolutions,* 2nd edn. Chicago: University of Chicago Press, 1970.

Kukla, André. *Social Constructivism and the Philosophy of Science.* London and New York: Routledge, 2000.

Latour, Bruno. "Ramses II, est-il mort de la tuberculose?" La Recherche, 307 (March, 1998).

—— and Steve Woolgar. *Laboratory Life: The Social Construction of Scientific Facts.* Beverly Hills, Calif.: Sage Publications, 1979.

Lennon, Kathleen. "Feminist Epistemology as Local Epistemology." *Proceedings of the Aristotelian Society, Supplementary Volume* 71 (1997): 37–54.

Nagel, Thomas. *The Last Word.* Oxford: Oxford University Press, 1997.

—— "The Sleep of Reason." *The New Republic,* October 12, 1998, 32–8.

Pickering, Andrew. *Constructing Quarks: A Sociological History of Particle Physics.* Chicago: University of Chicago Press, 1984.

Putnam, Hilary. *Realism with a Human Face.* Cambridge, Mass.: Harvard University Press, 1990.

Quine, W. V. O. "Truth by Convention." In his *The Ways of Paradox and Other Essays.* Cambridge, Mass.: Harvard University Press, 1966.

Rorty, Richard. "Mind-Body Identity, Privacy, and Categories." *Review of Metaphysics* 19 (1965): 24–54.

—— *Philosophy and the Mirror of Nature.* Princeton: Princeton University Press, 1981.

—— "Does Academic Freedom have Philosophical Presuppositions: Academic Freedom and the Future of the University." *Academe* 80, no. 6 (November-December 1994).

—— *Truth and Progress, Philosophical Papers, Volume 3.* New York: Cambridge University Press, 1998.

—— *Philosophy and Social Hope.* New York: Penguin, 1999.

Searle, John. *The Construction of Social Reality.* New York: The Free Press, 1995.

Shapin, Steven and Simon Schaffer. *Leviathan and the Air-Pump: Hobbes, Boyle, and the Experimental Life.* Princeton: Princeton University Press, 1985.

Sokal, Alan. "Transgressing the Boundaries: Towards a Transformative Hermeneutics of Quantum Gravity." *Social Text* 46/7 (1996): 217–52.

—— and Jean Bricmont. *Fashionable Nonsense: Postmodern Intellectuals' Abuse of Science*. New York: Picador USA, 1998.

Stroud, Barry. "Wittgenstein and Logical Necessity." In his *Meaning, Understanding and Practice: Philosophical Essays*, 1–16. Oxford: Oxford University Press, 2000.

The Editors of *Lingua Franca*, ed., *The Sokal Hoax: The Sham that Shook the Academy*. Lincoln, Nebr.: University of Nebraska Press, 2000.

White, Roger. "Epistemic Permissiveness." *Philosophical Perspectives*, forthcoming.

Wittgenstein, Ludwig. *Philosophical Investigations*, trans. G. E. M. Anscombe. Oxford: Blackwell, 1953.

—— *On Certainty*, ed. G. E. M. Anscombe and G. H. von Wright, trans. Denis Paul and G. E. M. Anscombe. Oxford: Basil Blackwell, 1975.

Wittgenstein, Ludwig. *Remarks on the Foundations of Mathematics*, rev. edn., ed. G. H. von Wright, R. Rhees and G. E. M. Anscombe, trans. G.E.M. Anscombe. Cambridge, Mass.: The MIT Press, 1978.

INDEX

Thompson, J. J. 2

underdetermination 118, 125
universality:
   of facts 12–13
   of justification 13–16

White, R. 101, 110
Wittgenstein, L. 7, 69–70, 78, 80,
   108–9
Woolgar, S. 113

Zimmerman, L. 2